D1632333

993440197 5

GUILTY PLEASURES

Matt Tebbutt's
GUILTY
PLEASURES

YOUR FAVOURITE SWEET & SAVOURY
INDULGENCES IN 130 EASY RECIPES

Quercus

CONTENTS

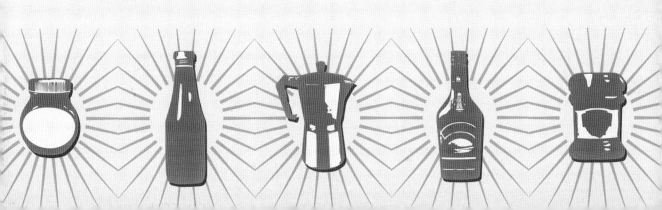

INTRODUCTION

Guilty pleasures – we all have them. For some, it's dancing around the living room to Abba. For others, it's lounging in bed all weekend. For me, and I suspect a lot of you, guilty pleasures tend to centre around food. We've all been caught with our spoon in the peanut butter one time or another, right? But as they say, a little bit of what you fancy does you good – so there is no reason to be ashamed of our secret food indulgences, as long as we keep a handle on things!

Like most chefs, I spend an awful lot of time banging the drum for local and seasonal foods, for organic this and free-range that – we build our professional careers on it. But we also know that there is a time and a place for purely indulgent food moments. Truth be told, though, many foods that are thought of as guilty pleasures – like coffee, peanut butter, ketchup and cola – are actually common cooking ingredients even in professional kitchens. So what I hope to give you here are great, light-hearted recipes that feature some of your favourite indulgences, so that you can enjoy your guilty pleasures every day. Okay, almost every day.

Everything in this book is easy to prepare and made with popular ingredients that can be found in every supermarket, so lots of my dishes can be whipped up with what you already have stocked in your kitchen cupboards. I've tried to give you a great variety of recipes to suit all tastes so that this book can be used for both day-to-day cooking and entertaining alike.

In a world where we have so many serious things to worry about, a bit of mild indulgence shouldn't be one of them. Like all guilty pleasures, a little bit of sin has never really been a bad thing … has it?

Tip

Just one hint for cooking with peanut butter – don't overheat or it can split. If it does, whisk in a few drops of cold water and it should come back together, helping you avoid disaster.

PEANUT BUTTER

I'm not ashamed to admit that I'm a huge fan of peanut butter; it's rich in flavour and totally moreish. I have friends who sheepishly eat it straight from the jar. Okay, I do it too, and I suspect so do you … and why not? But as an ingredient in cooking it has so much more to offer in both sweet and savoury dishes. And the more I explore food from around the world, the more I realise that some of our best-loved dishes already use peanut butter liberally – take satay, for example. Or bang bang chicken. Try my versions of these on pages 20 and 16. But if it's the sweet stuff you're after, there's plenty of that here too. My favourite recipe in this chapter, in case you're interested, is the Chocolate and Peanut Butter Layer Cake on page 25; it's chewy, dense and bloody delicious. If you're a total peanut butter addict, serve it *à la mode* with the Peanut Butter Ice Cream on page 28.

Peanut & Sesame
PRAWN TOASTS

This is a very easy version of a favourite Chinese takeaway classic. When making your own at home, these toasts end up far less greasy and you can really pack on the sesame seeds – win, win!

Makes about 18 pieces

FOR THE PRAWN PASTE
400g raw tiger prawns, shells removed
1 tbsp finely chopped root ginger
1 tsp salt
1 tbsp crushed garlic
Pinch of sugar
1 tsp soy sauce
2 tsp dry sherry
100g smooth peanut butter

FOR THE TOASTS
6 slices of white bread
100g sesame seeds, in shallow bowl

Oil, for frying
Finely shredded spring onions, to garnish

FOR THE SPICY CUCUMBER DIP
1 tsp sugar
½ tsp salt
200ml white wine or rice wine vinegar
5 tbsp fish sauce
2 fiery red chillies, seeded and finely chopped
¼ cucumber, finely diced

* First make the cucumber dip by simply mixing all the ingredients in a bowl. Taste and adjust as you prefer, adding more sugar, chilli, fish sauce, etc. Set aside.

* Next make the prawn paste. If you own a kitchen blender this is a doddle – throw all the paste ingredients into it and quickly blitz to combine; otherwise, blend using a pestle and mortar.

* Cut the crusts off the bread, then spread the paste over the slices quite thickly (more generously than you get in the local Chinese!). Cut each piece of bread into three strips. Press the coated bread strips, paste-side down, into the bowl of sesame seeds to liberally coat in seeds.

* Heat some oil in a frying pan over a medium to high heat, and fry the toasts on both sides for a few minutes, until golden brown. Remove, drain on kitchen paper, and serve with the spicy cucumber dip and shredded spring onions.

Roast Marinated
RACK OF LAMB
WITH A PEANUT AND YOGHURT DRESSING

We all need to indulge ourselves once in a while, and this special-occasion dish is ideal for extravagant Sundays or indeed any time you have guests. It's rather Middle-Eastern in its approach, the peanut butter adding a nice extra flavour dimension that contrasts well with the punchy spices and soothing yoghurt.

Serves 2

2 x 300g racks of lamb
Salt and pepper

FOR THE MARINADE
4 garlic cloves, crushed
2 tsp ground cumin
1 tbsp harissa paste
2 tbsp olive oil
Juice of ½ a lemon

FOR THE COUSCOUS
240g couscous
300ml hot lamb stock
Pinch of salt
Drizzle of olive oil
Pinch of allspice

Small bunch of fresh mint, chopped
Small bunch of fresh flat-leaf parsley, chopped
½ red onion, finely chopped
Grated zest of 1 lemon
50g toasted flaked almonds, crushed

FOR THE PEANUT YOGHURT DRESSING
2 tbsp smooth peanut butter
6 tbsp Greek yoghurt
1 tbsp chopped fresh mint
1 garlic clove, crushed
Juice of ½ a lemon
Salt and pepper

* Slash the racks of lamb in criss-crosses along the fat and skin, then season with salt and pepper.

* Combine all the marinade ingredients in a bowl and rub this paste generously all over the lamb. Put the meat in the fridge to marinate for 3 hours or more.

* Preheat the oven to 220°C/200°C fan/Gas 7.

* Put the meat in a roasting tin and blast in the oven for 20–25 minutes, depending on how pink you like it. Remove from the oven and allow to rest for 10 minutes, covered with foil, while you make the couscous and dressing. ➡

➡ CONTINUED FROM OVERLEAF

* Place the couscous in a large bowl and pour in the hot stock. Add a big pinch of salt, cover the bowl with cling film and let it sit for 10 minutes.

* Meanwhile, make the dressing by mixing the peanut butter with the yoghurt, mint and garlic. Season with salt and pepper and add a squeeze of lemon juice.

* Uncover the couscous and run a fork through the grains to fluff them up. Drizzle in some olive oil and stir in all the remaining couscous ingredients. Chuck away any big lumps of couscous that have stuck together. Taste and season with salt and pepper as necessary.

* To serve, slice the lamb racks and lay them on top of a big pile of the couscous, spoon over the meat juices and dollop on the peanut yoghurt dressing. Crack open a big bottle of red, sit down and enjoy.

Chilli & Mascarpone
PEANUT DIP

This sweet-and-savoury dip is easy, fridge-standby stuff, the sort of thing that cookbooks say is 'perfect for serving up to unexpected guests'. And it is! It's delicious served simply with raw vegetables as a canapé or starter.

Feeds 6

60g mascarpone cheese
250g smooth peanut butter
1 tsp coriander seeds, toasted and crushed
1 small green chilli, diced
Splash of milk or double cream, to loosen
Salt and pepper

TO SERVE
1 cucumber, cut into batons
1 cauliflower, broken into florets
150g cooked green beans
4 carrots, cut into batons
350g cooked new potatoes

* In a bowl, mix the mascarpone with the peanut butter, coriander seeds and chilli (with or without the seeds, depending on how spicy you like it).

* Season with salt and pepper and loosen the consistency with a splash of milk or cream. Serve with the selection of vegetables listed above, for dipping.

Bang Bang
CHICKEN SALAD

Bang bang chicken is a popular Chinese dish of shredded chicken dressed with a spicy sesame sauce and served on a bed of crisp salad. I've added peanut butter to the mix to make it even more delicious. This is one of my favourite dishes, and such a crowd-pleaser. The stock the chicken is cooked in is fantastic saved for soup, so it's thrifty to boot!

Serves 4–6

1 medium-sized chicken

Cos lettuce leaves and shredded carrot, cucumber and spring onions, to serve

Sesame seeds, coriander leaves and chilli oil, to garnish

FOR THE PEANUT SAUCE
250g peanut butter

2 tbsp toasted sesame oil

1 tbsp soy sauce

Juice of 1 lemon

Chilli oil or sauce, to taste

FOR THE STOCK
1 small lump of fresh root ginger, peeled and chopped

1 head of garlic, cut through the middle

Bunch of coriander stalks

2 tsp coriander seeds

1 star anise

1 whole red chilli

2 lemongrass stalks or a few slices of lemon

* Put the chicken in a large saucepan or cooking pot with all the stock ingredients and add enough cold water to cover. Bring to the boil over a high heat, then turn down to a very gentle simmer and cook for around 1 hour, skimming the surface of the liquid occasionally to remove any scum that rises up. Turn off the heat and allow the chicken to cool a little in the stock.

* Make the peanut sauce by whisking a little of the warm chicken broth with the peanut butter and all the other ingredients until you have a runny consistency. Taste and adjust the flavourings as necessary.

* When the chicken is cool enough to handle, remove from the stock and pull it apart into shreds. Arrange the lettuce, carrot, cucumber and spring onions on plates, scatter the shredded meat on top and spoon on generous amounts of the warm peanut sauce. Garnish with sesame seeds, coriander leaves and a drizzle of chilli oil.

Matt's Peanut
GUMBO

Gumbo is a thick stew typically made with okra and prawns. This isn't the classic recipe but my choice of ingredients means it's more of a gumbo than a soup. It's rich, warming and very, very filling, and the combination of flavours and textures works a treat.

Serves 4

FOR THE GUMBO
Olive oil, for frying
1 onion, diced
3 garlic cloves, chopped
2 green peppers, seeded and diced
2 tsp hot smoked paprika
1 green chilli, chopped
1 x 400g can chopped tomatoes
1 x 400ml can coconut milk
250g okra
800g raw prawns
150g cured sausage, sliced
100g crunchy peanut butter

Bunch of fresh coriander, chopped
Thai fish sauce (optional but
adds a fishy depth)
Juice of 1 lime
Salt and pepper

FOR THE TOMATO SALSA
5 tomatoes, seeded and diced
1 red onion, diced
Splash of red wine vinegar
1 garlic clove, crushed
A few sprigs of thyme, leaves picked
Pinch of salt
Drizzle of olive oil

* First make the salsa. Mix the tomatoes and red onion with the vinegar, crushed garlic, thyme leaves and salt. Leave for 30 minutes to draw out the tomato juices, then add olive oil to taste. Set aside.

* Heat a film of olive oil in a large frying pan over a medium heat and throw in the onion, garlic and peppers. Cook for 10 minutes to soften. Add the smoked paprika and chilli. Chuck in the tomatoes and cook for 5 minutes, then pour in the coconut milk. Add the whole okra and simmer the gumbo, uncovered, for 10 minutes to thicken slightly.

* Add the prawns and sliced sausage and poach gently for another 10 minutes.

* Remove from the heat and stir in the peanut butter, then add the chopped coriander and season with salt, pepper, the fish sauce (if using) and the lime juice. Serve the gumbo with the tomato salsa alongside.

Latin American
PEANUT SOUP

This soup and variations of it can be found all over Latin America. Each country has its own twist – some with potatoes, others with more chilli or peanuts, and some finished with avocado or chopped hard-boiled eggs. Feel free to mix and match as you please.

Serves 4

50ml olive oil

1 red onion, diced

2 red peppers, seeded and diced

2 large red chillies, or chipotle (if you can get them), chopped

1 x 400g can chopped plum tomatoes

1.2 litres hot chicken stock

1 tsp Marmite (optional, but adds a beefy depth)

1 x 300g jar peanut butter, smooth or crunchy

Small bunch of fresh coriander, chopped, to serve

Soured cream, to serve

* Warm the oil in a large saucepan over a medium heat. Add the onion and peppers and cook for 20 minutes or so, until soft. Add the chopped chillies, seeds and all, then the tomatoes. Pour in the stock and the Marmite (if using) and simmer for another 20 minutes.

* Remove from the heat and stir in the peanut butter until well blended. Serve the soup in bowls with chopped coriander scattered over and a dollop of soured cream stirred through.

PORK SATAY

This popular, peanutty starter is simple and failsafe to make at home. The description 'satay' really refers to the way the meat is marinated and then grilled or cooked over hot coals, rather than the sauce itself. Peanut has become the norm for satay, but cucumber and pineapple are also popular throughout Asia. You can also make this with chicken, of course.

Serves 4

2 pork tenderloins (about 400g in total), cut into bite-sized chunks

Red onion and cucumber chunks, and sliced red chilli, to serve

FOR THE PEANUT SAMBAL

100g peanut butter, smooth or crunchy

1 tbsp chilli sauce

1 tbsp sesame oil

1 garlic clove, chopped

2–3 tbsp soy sauce

Juice of 1 lime

A little milk, to loosen

FOR THE MARINADE

1 garlic clove, minced

1 tsp minced ginger

1 tbsp soy sauce

1 tbsp honey

2 lemongrass stalks, crushed and finely chopped

Bunch of fresh coriander, chopped

2 tsp Thai fish sauce

Olive oil, to loosen

* First, combine all the marinade ingredients in a bowl, adding enough oil to loosen the consistency. Throw in the chunks of pork, coat them in the mixture, and allow to marinate in the fridge for 30 minutes.

* Meanwhile, mix together all the ingredients for the peanut sambal in a small bowl, adding just enough milk to loosen the sauce.

* Heat the grill or barbecue. Skewer the pork pieces on lemongrass sticks or pre-soaked wooden skewers and grill for 15–20 minutes on a high heat, turning them halfway through, until the meat is cooked through. Serve with the peanut sambal, some red onion and cucumber chunks, and sliced red chilli.

Peanut Butter & Raisin
BLONDIES

Blondies make an irresistible alternative to the classic chocolate brownie (though don't miss my recipe for those on page 106). These are rich and decadent – and even more delicious if you throw a handful of white chocolate buttons into the mix.

Makes 18

300g crunchy peanut butter
200g butter, soft, plus extra for greasing
340g light brown sugar
2 eggs, beaten

1 tsp vanilla extract
200g golden raisins
260g plain flour
2 tsp baking powder
50ml milk

* Preheat the oven to 160°C/140°C fan/Gas 2. Grease a 35 x 25cm baking tin with butter and line with baking paper (or use a non-stick tin).

* In a mixing bowl, beat together the peanut butter and soft butter until smooth. Stir in the sugar, beaten eggs, vanilla extract and raisins. Gently fold in the flour and baking powder, and stir in enough of the milk that the mixture is just loose enough to pour.

* Tip the mixture into the prepared baking tin. Bake in the oven for 25–35 minutes, until the blondies are risen with a golden crust. Allow to cool completely in the tin before slicing.

Chocolate & Peanut Butter
LAYER CAKE

This is layer upon layer of luxury itself – delicious peanut butter cream sandwiched between rich chocolate sponge. What more could anyone want from a cake?!

Serves 8–10

FOR THE SPONGE
300g dark chocolate, broken up
350g butter, soft, plus extra for greasing
350g caster sugar
6 eggs, beaten
350g self-raising flour
2 tsp baking powder
8 tbsp cocoa powder
A little milk, if necessary

FOR THE FROSTING
400g smooth peanut butter
400g icing sugar
70g butter, soft
100g soured cream

FOR THE PEANUT BRITTLE
150g caster sugar
100g roasted peanuts

* Preheat the oven to 180°C/160°C fan/Gas 4. Grease three 20cm, round cake tins with butter and line with baking paper (or use non-stick tins).

* For the sponge, melt the chocolate in a heatproof bowl set over a saucepan of simmering water, stirring frequently. When melted, remove from the heat and set aside for the chocolate to cool a little.

* In a mixing bowl, beat the butter with the sugar for 10 minutes until soft. Mix in the beaten eggs bit by bit, then gently fold in the flour, baking powder and cocoa. If the mixture feels stiff, add some milk to slacken it. Stir in the cooled runny chocolate, then tip the mixture into the prepared tins. Bake for 25–30 minutes until the cakes are risen and springy. Leave to cool in the tins a little, then transfer to a wire rack to cool fully.

* Meanwhile, make the peanut brittle. Line a baking tray with greaseproof paper. Melt the sugar in a frying pan over a high heat for a few minutes, keeping a close eye on it, until it becomes a golden caramel. Remove from the heat and stir in the peanuts, then pour immediately into the lined baking tray. Allow to cool completely and then break into chunks.

➡ CONTINUED FROM OVERLEAF

∗ For the frosting, beat the peanut butter with the icing sugar and butter until smooth. Beat in the soured cream, taste, then adjust the sweetness if necessary with a little more icing sugar.

∗ When the cakes have cooled, place one on a plate or cake stand and spread with some of the frosting. Top with another cake layer, more frosting, then the final layer of cake. Frost the top of the cake, using a piping bag if you wish. Make it sexy! Finally, decorate with shards of the peanut brittle.

Chocolate Peanut Butter
TRUFFLES

Rich, dark and satisfying, these salty-sweet treats are a perfect accompaniment to after-dinner coffee, or gobbled at any time of the day, truth be told. The big spoonful of peanut butter provides an extra richness that will delight and surprise. This recipe makes quite a few truffles but they freeze very well for another time.

Makes about 15–20

250g dark chocolate, broken up
75ml double cream
75g smooth peanut butter
Cocoa powder or finely chopped peanuts, for coating

* Place the chocolate and cream in a small saucepan over a medium heat. Allow to melt, stirring until combined. Remove from the heat and stir in the peanut butter. Scrape into a bowl, cover with cling film and chill until hard.

* When set, use a small spoon or melon baller to take scoops of the mixture and mould into balls. Place the cocoa powder or finely chopped peanuts on a small plate and roll the balls of mixture across the plate to coat. Serve with coffee.

Peanut Butter
ICE CREAM

You *have* to try this little number – the most delicious, no-churn ice cream ever! It's incredibly smooth and soft-set and has a similar taste to salted caramel. Make into retro ice cream sandwiches with the Peanut Butter and Raisin Cookies on page 31. You need a sugar thermometer for this recipe.

Serves 4–6

170g caster sugar
12 egg yolks
250g smooth peanut butter
200ml double cream, whipped to soft peaks

* Put the sugar and 6 tablespoons of water in a sturdy saucepan and place over a medium heat. Allow to boil, without stirring, until it reaches 116°C on a sugar thermometer (known as the soft-ball stage).

* Meanwhile, begin whisking the egg yolks in a freestanding mixer or using an electric hand-held whisk.

* When the sugar reaches the right temperature, immediately remove from the heat and pour it very carefully into the eggs, with the mixer or whisk still running. Be careful not to splash as the sugar will be very hot! Continue whisking until it is totally cool, then mix in the peanut butter and fold in the whipped cream.

* Pour the mixture into a suitable container and freeze, preferably overnight or for at least 8 hours, until ready for scooping.

Peanut Butter & Raisin
COOKIES

These will keep for a few days in a cookie jar but, to be honest, I doubt they'll even get as far as the jar. They are best eaten warm from the oven, on your own, so as not to have to share them. They're also pretty good sandwiched around the Peanut Butter Ice Cream on page 28. If you do this, let the cookies cool first, for obvious reasons.

Makes 12–15

60g peanut butter, smooth or crunchy
50g salted butter, soft
100g light brown sugar
1 egg, beaten
100g plain flour
1 tbsp baking powder
50g raisins

* Preheat the oven to 180°C/160°C fan/Gas 4. In a large bowl, mix together the peanut butter, soft butter and sugar, until smooth. Add the egg and mix to combine, then gently fold in the flour, baking powder and raisins.

* Roll heaped tablespoonfuls of the mixture into balls and place on a non-stick baking sheet, spaced apart.

* Bake in the oven for around 10 minutes until golden brown. They may be a little soft in the centre when you take them out of the oven, but when cool they will be the perfect mix of chewy and slightly crunchy. Cool, eat, done!

PEANUT BUTTER & PECAN PIE

This is my twist on the original and delicious American classic. It's well worth the calories, I'm telling you.

Serves 8–10

FOR THE PASTRY
150g salted butter, chilled, plus extra for greasing
2 egg yolks
55g caster sugar
300g plain flour, plus extra for dusting

FOR THE FILLING
6 eggs
45g light brown sugar

125ml maple syrup
1 tsp vanilla extract
75g peanut butter, smooth or crunchy
270g pecan nuts

TO SERVE (OPTIONAL)
200ml double cream
Icing sugar, to taste
5 tbsp whisky

* First make the pastry, by whizzing the butter with the egg yolks and sugar in a food processor to make a paste. Then add the flour and stop mixing as soon as it all comes together. Wrap the pastry in cling film and chill for 30 minutes.

* Preheat the oven to 180°C/160°C fan/Gas 4. Grease a 24cm round tart tin with a removable base and line with baking paper (or use a non-stick tin).

* Unwrap the pastry and roll out on a lightly floured surface, then use it to line the tart tin. Prick the pastry all over with a fork, and place a circle of baking parchment in the base. Pour in baking beans (or dried beans) to hold the paper in place.

* Bake the pastry case for 15–20 minutes until just turning golden. Remove the beans and paper, then cook for another 10 minutes. Remove from the oven, leaving it turned on but reducing the temperature to 150°C/130°C fan/Gas 2.

* For the filling, beat the eggs with the sugar, maple syrup, vanilla extract and peanut butter. Stir in the pecans, and pour everything into the cooked pastry case. Bake for 25–30 minutes, until the top is firm to the touch. Leave to cool before cutting into slices.

* If you fancy some whisky cream on the side, whip the double cream with a sprinkling of icing sugar and the whisky, until soft peaks form. Dollop some next to the pie to make this a winner!

Peanut Caramel
POACHED PEARS

What better way to enjoy one of your five-a-day than doused in peanut caramel sauce! Keep the poaching liquor from these pears to use again, or for poaching other fruits. It'll sit quite happily in a sealed container in the fridge for weeks.

Serves 4

4 just-ripe pears

1 x 75cl bottle white wine (or water, if you must)

1 star anise

A few cloves and peppercorns

1 cinnamon stick

1 vanilla pod

Grated zest of 1 lemon

150g caster sugar

FOR THE PEANUT CARAMEL

150g caster sugar

150–175ml double cream

100g crunchy peanut butter

* Peel the pears and carefully scoop out the core at the base only. Bring the wine or water to the boil in a medium saucepan over a high heat, with the spices, lemon zest and sugar. Reduce the heat and simmer for 10 minutes to infuse.

* Drop the pears into the pan. If their tops are sticking out, top up the pan with a little water. Cover with a plate or lid and bring back up to the boil, then simmer for 5 minutes or so. Turn off the heat and allow the pears to cool (and carry on cooking) in the liquor.

* Meanwhile, make the peanut caramel. Tip the sugar into a dry, medium saucepan and set it over a high heat – keep an eye on it at all times, as the sugar won't take long to change colour. Don't stir, but swirl the pan a bit to move the molten caramel, and when all the sugar has turned a rich brown colour, remove from the heat and tip in the double cream. Stir together, being careful not to splash, and don't be tempted to stick your fingers in the pan – you'll lose them!

* When the caramel is cool, stir in the peanut butter. If the mixture splits and looks greasy, stir in a little cold water and all should be well.

* To serve, simply arrange the pears on plates, drizzle with the peanut caramel – and that's it!

Mini Peanut Butter
BAKED ALASKAS

This involves a few different stages of work, but it's so spectacular and wonderfully kitsch that you should definitely give it a go.

Makes 4

FOR THE CAKE
40g salted butter, soft, plus extra for greasing
50g crunchy peanut butter
70g caster sugar
30g light brown sugar
1 large egg, beaten
125g self-raising flour
¼ tsp baking powder
Pinch of salt
2–3 tbsp milk, plus a splash

FOR THE ALASKA TOPPING
1-litre tub chocolate or vanilla ice cream (or your favourite flavour)
3 egg whites
Pinch of salt
75g caster sugar

* Preheat the oven to 200°C/180°C fan/Gas 6. Grease an 18cm square cake tin and line with baking paper (or use a non-stick tin).

* For the cake, beat together the soft butter and peanut butter in a mixing bowl, then blend in the sugars and egg. Gently fold in the flour, baking powder and salt, and loosen the mixture with a little milk.

* Tip the mixture into the prepared tin and bake for 30–35 minutes until risen and springy. Leave to cool in the tin a little, then transfer to a wire rack to cool fully. Once cool, trim the edges of the cake and cut into four rectangular slices.

* Meanwhile, remove the ice cream from the freezer and leave to soften slightly. Once the cake has been removed from the tin, wash it out and line with cling film. Spoon the softened ice cream into the lined tin and press down firmly so it's about 2cm deep. Put back in the freezer for 30–40 minutes to harden up.

* Now prepare the meringue. Whisk the egg whites with the salt in a large, clean bowl. Gradually add the sugar, continuing to whisk until the whites are glossy and doubled in volume. Scrape the mixture into a piping bag with a plain nozzle.

* When the ice cream has frozen, cut it into slices the same size as your cakes. Place the ice cream slices on the cake slices, pipe on the meringue and carefully brown it with a cook's torch. Rush them to the table before they start melting!

Ketchup and mustard are doubtless the most reached-for condiments on the table, but they're usually just supporting acts to a meal. Not any more! They can add a wonderful dimension to food when they're not just hanging around on the side of a plate. You might sniff at your friends who put ketchup all over their meat (which of course YOU never do … much), but in all seriousness, maybe they know something you don't. The sugar, spices and vinegar in ketchup can produce deliciously rich results, especially when used in barbecue cooking or as a glaze – give my legendary Slow-Cooked Pulled Pork a whirl (see page 48). Meanwhile, mustard is a great way to ramp up the heat without going the whole hog and wheeling out the chillies. Grainy mustard adds a nutty crunch, and a spoonful of Dijon is an instant route to silky and sophisticated sauces. Michelin-starred kitchens have been using these two characters in their food forever – so if it's okay with them, it's okay with me. When it comes to desserts, however, that's a different story and, for me, a step too far no matter how much you love the stuff. So if chocolate mustard muffins is what you're after, forget it! You won't find them here.

KETCHUP
&
MUSTARD

Salmon & Ginger
FISHCAKES
WITH WASABI MAYONNAISE

Most fishcake recipes contain potato but I've deliberately left it out of mine in favour of packing in even more fish! The mustard element here is actually wasabi, which comes from the roots of a plant in the same family as mustard. It gives a real punch to the mayonnaise, something that an ordinary mustard just can't compete with.

Serves 4 as a starter

FOR THE FISHCAKES

4 x 150g skinless salmon fillets, finely diced

1 garlic clove, finely crushed

4 spring onions, finely sliced

Small knob of fresh root ginger, peeled and grated

Juice of 1 lime

1 small green chilli, seeded and finely chopped

Small splash of dry sherry

Oil, for frying

Salt and pepper

FOR THE SALAD

½ a mooli or Japanese white radish, finely sliced

½ cucumber, finely sliced

Handful of red breakfast radishes, finely sliced

1 tbsp caster sugar

3 tbsp white wine vinegar

Lemon halves or wedges, to serve

FOR THE WASABI MAYONNAISE

4 tbsp mayonnaise

Wasabi paste, to taste

* In a large bowl, mix together all the fishcake ingredients except the oil, then season with salt and pepper and leave in the fridge to marinate for 30 minutes. Form into small patties and chill for another 30 minutes to help bind together.

* Meanwhile, mix the mayonnaise with as much of the wasabi as you fancy, but it needs to be good and spicy! Set aside.

* For the salad, arrange the mooli, cucumber and radish slices on plates. Dissolve the sugar in the vinegar to make a dressing, and drizzle over the top.

* Heat a little oil in a frying pan over a medium heat and fry the fishcakes for 3–4 minutes on each side until golden. You can, if you dare, serve them still slightly pink in the middle. To serve, place on the plates next to the salad, add lemon wedges and dollop some wasabi mayonnaise on the side.

Sweet & Sour
FISH

It's always worth the effort making these popular takeaway dishes at home, as you can play around with the flavours to suit your taste and create a sauce that you love (as opposed to that objectionable red gloop that you sometimes get with a takeaway). Ketchup is the secret to the sweetness here.

Enough for 4

FOR THE FISH

500g thick white fish, such as cod, haddock, pollock or halibut, cut into chunks

150ml vegetable oil

Cornflour, for dusting

2 onions, diced

2 red peppers, seeded and diced

2 carrots, sliced on an angle

4 spring onions, chopped

150g tomato ketchup

2–3 tbsp white wine vinegar

400g fresh pineapple, diced

Rice or noodles, to serve

FOR THE MARINADE

2 tbsp soy sauce

2 tbsp white wine

1 garlic clove, grated

Small knob of fresh root ginger, grated

Generous pinch of Chinese five spice

* Combine all the ingredients for the marinade in a bowl, add the fish and leave in the fridge to marinate for 30 minutes.

* Heat the oil in a pan or wok. Remove the fish from the marinade (reserving the marinade itself for later), pat dry and dust with the cornflour. Throw into the hot pan and cook for a few minutes on a medium heat, until starting to colour on all sides. Remove and drain on kitchen paper.

* Pour off most of the oil from the pan, throw in the vegetables and cook over a low heat for 10 minutes. Stir in the ketchup, vinegar and the reserved marinade. Allow to simmer for a few minutes then add the fresh pineapple.

* Now return the fish to the pan and simmer very gently for 10 minutes until cooked through. Serve with rice or noodles.

Butter-Poached
HERRING FILLETS
WITH CHIVE AND MUSTARD SAUCE

American hot-dog mustard is sweet and smooth – and it's been a guilty pleasure of mine for some time now. In this seriously fast and delicious dish it helps to balance the sour notes that come from curing the fish.

Serves 2

FOR THE POACHED FISH
6 fresh herring fillets
100g salted butter
125ml white wine
150ml water
A couple of lemon slices
A few sprigs of fresh dill or chives
1 tsp sugar
1 tsp white wine vinegar

FOR THE CHIVE AND MUSTARD SAUCE
200g French's American mustard
100g mayonnaise
50ml white wine vinegar
½ bunch fresh chives, finely chopped
Salt and pepper

* Place the fish and all the poaching ingredients together in a large saucepan, cover with a lid, and poach very gently over a low heat for 4–6 minutes or until the fish is cooked through.

* Meanwhile, to make the sauce, mix together the mustard, mayo and vinegar. Stir in the chives and season with salt and pepper.

* Lift the cooked fish out of the poaching liquid with a slotted spoon and serve with a generous spoonful of the chive and mustard sauce.

CAULIFLOWER, BACON & CHICORY SOUP

WITH DIJON MUSTARD

I've thrown a decent amount of bacon into this mustardy soup, but you can always leave it out if it's not your thing: there's enough flavour going on even without. The Dijon brings a silky warmth to the soup, rather than a powerful kick. Any other mustard would overpower.

Serves 4

50g salted butter

2 tbsp olive oil

8 rashers of streaky bacon, chopped

2 garlic cloves, chopped

1 onion, diced

2 heads red or white chicory, thick end removed and diced, leaves shredded

2 small heads cauliflower, roughly chopped

500ml hot vegetable stock or water

500ml milk

100g cream cheese

100g Cheddar cheese, grated

1 tbsp Dijon mustard

100g blue cheese, crumbled, to serve

Salt and pepper

* Preheat the oven to 200°C/180°C fan/Gas 6.

* Heat the butter and 1 tablespoon of the oil in a large ovenproof saucepan or flameproof casserole over a high heat, then throw in six of the chopped rashers of bacon and cook until coloured. Add the garlic and onion and the diced chicory ends and cook over a low heat for 10 minutes to soften.

* Stir in the cauliflower and cook gently for another 10 minutes without letting the veg colour. Now add the stock (or water) and the milk – the top of the vegetables should be sticking out of the liquid. Place the whole pot in the oven without the lid and cook for 40 minutes to start getting some colour on top.

* Meanwhile, fry the remaining bacon in the rest of the olive oil, until crispy.

* When the cauliflower starts to brown and look roasted, remove and blitz everything with a hand-held blender or in a food processor. Taste, season with salt and pepper, and strain into a clean pan. Stir in the cream cheese, Cheddar cheese and Dijon mustard.

* Serve with the crumbled blue cheese, reserved crispy bacon and shredded chicory leaves scattered over.

Mackerel TERIYAKI

Teriyaki is the Japanese name given to meat or fish that has been marinated in a sweet sauce and then grilled. Teriyaki relies on sweetness to create a glaze and this where the ketchup comes into its own. I'm using mackerel here but chicken, squid or salmon would work just as well.

Serves 4 as a starter

100ml dark soy sauce
2 tbsp ketchup
1 tbsp lemon juice
1 tbsp grated fresh root ginger
1 garlic clove, crushed
1 tbsp white wine vinegar
4 mackerel fillets, pin boned
Bok choy and spring onions,
chopped and blanched, to serve

* Simply mix everything together in a large bowl, except the fish, bok choy and spring onions. Taste and adjust the flavourings to your liking.

* Slip the mackerel fillets into the bowl of marinade and leave in the fridge for 20 minutes to become delicious.

* Heat your grill to its highest setting. Lift the fillets out of the marinade, place on a baking sheet and grill for 6–8 minutes. Keep an eye on the fish, as it can easily burn. Cook until the skin is crispy and golden and the flesh is cooked through. Serve with the blanched bok choy and spring onions.

Three-Mustard
DEVILLED KIDNEYS

To 'devil' something is to spice it up, and devilled kidneys are an old British classic. It's up to you how spicy you make them, but they may as well have punch or else they're not worth making. I've used three types of mustard here, so go wild!

Serves 4

6 tbsp plain flour
2 tbsp English mustard powder
1 tbsp cayenne pepper
1 tsp salt
1 tsp black pepper
600g lambs' kidneys
100ml double cream
Splash of Worcestershire sauce
1 tbsp Dijon mustard
1 tsp wholegrain mustard
50g butter
Hot toast, to serve

* Mix the flour in a bowl with the mustard powder, cayenne, salt and pepper.

* Cut the kidneys in half lengthways and then remove the white core using a pair of scissors. Dust the kidneys in the seasoned flour.

* Combine the cream, Worcestershire sauce, Dijon and wholegrain mustard in a saucepan and bring to the boil over a high heat. Once boiling, remove the pan from the heat.

* Melt the butter in a large frying pan over a medium heat. Add the kidneys and fry gently for no more than 3–4 minutes in total, turning halfway through. Remove from the pan, allow to rest somewhere warm for a minute or two, then put them on plates, spoon over the mustardy cream and serve with hot toast.

Slow-Cooked
PULLED PORK

Pulled pork is basically a joint that has been cooked slowly and for such a long time that you can literally pull it apart with your fingers. It's an American stalwart and there are lots of different recipes and methods for cooking it, but the sauce is always sticky, sweet and slightly sour and spicy. It's everything I love about food. The ketchup in my version adds sweetness and a delicious tomatoey tang. You need to start this a day in advance and allow lots of time for cooking.

Serves 8–10

FOR THE PULLED PORK

2kg pork shoulder
100g fine sea salt
150g light brown sugar
1 tbsp cayenne pepper
1 tbsp smoked paprika
1 tbsp ground cumin
½ tbsp black pepper
200g tomato ketchup
2 tbsp white wine vinegar
4 garlic cloves, crushed
4 tbsp soy sauce
1 lemon

TO SERVE

Sliced gherkins
Barbecue sauce
Fennel and Apple Mustardy Slaw (page 50)
Crusty bread

* Start by slashing the pork shoulder all over lightly and rub it generously and vigorously with the salt and sugar. Set aside in the fridge overnight.

* Next day, preheat the oven to 140°C/120°C fan/Gas 1. Wash the pork well to remove the salt and sugar and dry with kitchen paper.

* Mix together all the other ingredients, apart from the lemon. Rub this mixture all over the meat then whack the joint into the oven. Forget about it for 6–8 hours (the longer and slower the better!), but do baste it every now and again with any of the fat and marinade that comes from the meat. Towards the end of the cooking, squeeze the lemon all over the pork to give it a lift.

* Remove from the oven and leave to cool for a while, then literally pull the meat apart into slithers and chunks. Serve with the Fennel and Apple Mustardy Slaw (page 50), plus barbecue sauce, gherkins and crusty bread.

Fennel & Apple MUSTARDY SLAW

This is an interesting and more refreshing version of common slaw. It goes brilliantly with everything but try it with my Slow-Cooked Pulled Pork (see page 48) for a perfect pairing.

Enough for 4 people

2 tbsp mayonnaise

1 tbsp English mustard

Juice of 1 lemon

1 heaped tbsp Greek yoghurt

2 fennel bulbs, cut into super-thin slices and put in iced water

2 Cox's apples, cored and cut into batons

1 green chilli, seeded and finely sliced

1 red onion, sliced finely into semi-circles

1 tbsp chopped fresh dill

1 tbsp capers

* Mix the mayonnaise in a bowl with the mustard, lemon juice and yoghurt.

* Remove the fennel from the iced water and toss together with the apples, chilli, onion, dill and capers. Add enough of the mayonnaise mixture to just bind everything together.

* Serve straight away, while the slaw is still fresh and crisp.

SLOPPY JOES

A slightly unappetizing name for what is essentially a very loose-textured burger – so loose, in fact, that it fills your hands with mince when you eat it. Apparently invented by a man called Joe in 1930s Iowa, it's become one of the great American classics. It's made with both ketchup and mustard, making it perfect diner food at home

Makes 4 burgers

Oil, for frying

500g minced beef

1 red and 1 green pepper, seeded and diced

1 onion, diced

2 celery sticks, diced

1 tbsp white wine or cider vinegar

2 tsp Dijon mustard

Generous splash of Worcestershire sauce

60ml tomato ketchup

1 x 400g can chopped tomatoes

TO SERVE

4 white burger buns, toasted

8 lettuce leaves

4 slices of red onion

2 ripe tomatoes, sliced

4 tbsp mayonnaise

(and lots of fries!)

* Place a little oil in a large frying pan over a high heat, then add the beef mince and cook until brown. When done, remove the meat from the pan and drain away most of the oil. Add the diced vegetables to the hot pan and cook for 10 minutes or so.

* Stir in the vinegar and mustard, and then mix in the browned meat. Add the Worcestershire sauce, ketchup and tomatoes and simmer for 10–15 minutes, until thick.

* Serve in the toasted burger baps with all the other bits and pieces and a heap of fries alongside.

Honey & Mustard
SEAFOOD KEBABS

Scallops and prawns are rather grand, but this recipe works well with other fish, too, if you're not feeling so flash. Try a couple of skinned plaice fillets or chunks of thick white fish, such as haddock or cod.

Serves 4

8 whole scallops
12 large prawns
3 tbsp extra virgin olive oil
1 tbsp chopped flat-leaf parsley
Juice of 1 lemon
Sea salt
Lemon wedges, to garnish

FOR THE MARINADE
2 tbsp runny honey
4 tbsp tomato ketchup
2 tsp Dijon mustard
4 tbsp soy sauce
2 tsp hot pepper sauce

* Mix all the marinade ingredients together, then toss in the scallops and prawns and leave in the fridge to marinate for 30 minutes. If using wooden skewers, soak them in water during this time so that they won't burn.

* Set the grill to a high heat. Thread the marinated seafood onto four skewers, arranging the scallops in the curve of the prawns if you can. Season with sea salt and drizzle the skewers with a tablespoon of the oil. Grill for 4–5 minutes on each side.

* Mix together the remaining olive oil, the chopped parsley and lemon juice and drizzle over the kebabs before serving with the lemon wedges.

Spicy Mustard
CHICKEN WINGS

Be warned: these are fiery! You may want to make more paste by adding extra mustard powder but you really don't need a lot for it to have an impact. If you find the wings start to brown too quickly in the oven, just cover them loosely with some foil and carry on.

Serves 4–6

3 heaped tbsp English mustard powder
4 tsp grated fresh root ginger
1 tsp black pepper
3 green chillies, seeded and finely chopped
Splash of white wine vinegar or rice wine vinegar
1kg chicken wings
Soured cream and coleslaw (page 50), to serve

* In a bowl, combine the mustard powder, ginger, pepper, chillies and enough of the vinegar to make a spreadable paste.

* Rub the paste all over the chicken wings and leave in the fridge to marinate for 1 hour.

* Preheat the oven to 180°C/160°C fan/Gas 4. Empty the chicken wings into a large roasting tray or ovenproof dish.

* Roast the chicken wings in the oven for 30 minutes until cooked through and golden. Serve with soured cream and coleslaw.

Classic
SAUCE BOIS BOUDRAN

This is a rather posh, restaurant-style sauce that's an absolute star. It's sweet and sour, tomatoey and bloody delicious, and is great with lamb or fish, or in fact just about anything. Served warm as an accompaniment it can elevate even the most mundane of dishes. You can make it, stick it in the fridge and forget about it; the longer you leave it, the better it tastes.

Enough for 6 servings

300ml mild-tasting oil, such as peanut or groundnut
50ml white wine vinegar
150g tomato ketchup

Tabasco sauce, to taste
4 shallots, diced
Chopped fresh herbs (such as tarragon, chives and parsley), to serve

* Combine the oil, vinegar and ketchup in a small saucepan and warm through gently over a low heat. Add Tabasco, to taste.

* Remove from the heat and stir through the diced shallots and chopped fresh herbs just before serving, so that they keep their colour and freshness. Serve warm, with your choice of meat or fish.

Spiced
DIPPING SAUCE

This makes a great barbecue sauce and can be used as a marinade for pork ribs or chicken. The sweetness of the ketchup helps balance the fiery Tabasco and salty soy.

Serves 4

150ml tomato ketchup
80ml orange juice
½ tsp Tabasco sauce, or more to taste
2 tbsp dark soy sauce

* Mix all the ingredients together and do a taste test. Adjust the flavourings if necessary. Use as required (see my suggestions above).

Marie Rose
DRESSING

Part of the classic prawn cocktail, this was the first sauce I learned to make in a busy, brutal Michelin-starred kitchen. I still get a bit of a nostalgic thrill when I throw it together. It's a beautifully balanced sweet and spicy, velvety sauce, although it is pink! Use this with a pinch of paprika in your prawn or seafood cocktail, with iceberg lettuce for a retro touch. Or try it with potato salad or even on chips.

Makes enough for 4

3 egg yolks (plus an extra one just in case)
1 tbsp Dijon mustard
100ml tomato ketchup
Pinch of salt
**300ml peanut or groundnut oil (basically
a mild-tasting oil – not olive!)**
Splash of brandy, to taste
Squeeze of lemon juice

* Drop the egg yolks into a large, clean bowl with the mustard, ketchup and a pinch of salt. Gradually whisk in the oil, being careful the mixture doesn't split. If it does, whisk up another yolk and add the split mixture to it very slowly.

* When the yolks have tripled in size and you have used all the oil, add the brandy to taste and a squeeze of lemon juice. Taste and adjust the seasoning, adding more salt or lemon juice – or indeed brandy, for an extra kick. Use as required.

COFFEE & TEA

Ah, your doctor told you not to drink so much, but you still have your daily mochaccino and five cups of builder's, don't you … Well, you can eat your vices, too, as both coffee and tea are easy to sneak into all kinds of recipes. Sweet coffee treats go without introduction, but it might be more of a surprise to find that coffee can also play centre-stage in savoury recipes. Its rich, earthy flavour works best in hearty food. Try it in the Wide-Awake Black Bean Chilli on page 62 for a memorable hit.

Tea offers even more options because there are so many different types. It's not used in many British dishes (yet!), but has been a mainstay of Far-Eastern recipes, both sweet and savoury, for eons. It adds a lovely, slightly bitter edge. Using it for home-smoking is lots of fun and results in unforgettable flavours – although it requires plenty of ventilation and an understanding landlord! See my recipe for Soy and Honey Smoked Chicken on page 71. Fragrant teas work well in cakes or with chocolate, while the Green Tea Pancakes on page 88 have to be tasted (and seen!) to be believed! There are a mind-boggling number of tea varieties, all with their own tastes and intensities, so have a go and experiment with the different flavours out there.

Wide-Awake
BLACK BEAN CHILLI
WITH TORTILLA CHIPS

This is called 'wide-awake' because of the espresso powder, which adds a subtle depth. What's not so subtle, however, is the heat – it's pretty fearsome in the chilli department, so reduce the quantities if you must!

Serves 4

Olive oil, for cooking
4 garlic cloves, sliced
2 red onions, sliced
2 red chillies, chopped
1 tsp chilli powder
2 tsp cumin seeds
1 tbsp dried oregano
1 tsp espresso powder
2 x 400g cans chopped tomatoes or 800g cherry tomatoes, halved
1 cinnamon stick

1 x 240g can cooked black beans, drained
1 x packet shop-bought tortilla wraps
Vegetable oil, for frying
Salt and pepper

TO SERVE
1–2 spring onions, chopped
Bunch of fresh coriander leaves
Lime wedges
Soured cream mixed with chopped mint leaves
Sliced jalapeño chillies

* Heat some olive oil in a large frying pan over a medium heat. Add the garlic and brown it lightly, then add the onions and cook gently for 10 minutes until soft. Add the chillies, chilli powder, cumin, oregano and espresso powder and cook for 1 minute, then throw in the tomatoes and cinnamon stick. Simmer for about 20 minutes until thickened slightly.

* Add the drained black beans and simmer for another 20 minutes. If it starts looking a little dry, just add a splash of water. When cooked, season the chilli mixture with salt and pepper and remove the cinnamon stick.

* Meanwhile, make the tortilla chips. Simply lay out the tortilla wraps and cut into triangles. Heat about 2cm vegetable oil in a large frying pan over a medium to high heat. When hot, throw in the triangles and cook until crisp and golden.

* Arrange the tortilla chips on a platter, dollop on the chilli, scatter over the chopped spring onion and garnish with fresh coriander. Serve with lime wedges and bowls of the minted soured cream and sliced jalapeño chillies.

Cowboy BRISKET

This is 'cowboy' because it was originally cooked over hot coals on Texan ranches. It's another American classic that marries coffee and meat – maybe the cowboys needed a pick-me-up! You need to start making this a day in advance to allow the meat plenty of time to marinate.

Feeds 6

6 garlic cloves, whole
1 tbsp brown sugar
1 tbsp ground black pepper
1 tbsp chilli powder
60ml cider vinegar

900g beef brisket
Olive oil, for frying
4 large onions, sliced
250ml strong black coffee
Salt and pepper

* In a large bowl, combine the garlic, sugar, pepper, chilli powder and vinegar. Sit the beef in the mixture and give the meat a good rub all over with it. Leave to marinate in the fridge overnight.

* The next day, pour a film of olive oil into the bottom of a large deep saucepan with a lid, and warm up over a high heat. Season the meat with salt and pepper and place it in the hot pan. Sear the beef on all sides then remove. Throw in the sliced onions and sauté for 10 minutes until softened. Pour in the coffee and bring to the boil.

* Put the brisket back in the pan and pour in 200ml of water. Cover with the lid and cook very slowly over a low heat on the hob, or alternatively transfer everything into an ovenproof casserole, cover, and cook in a low oven that's been preheated to 140°C/120°C fan/Gas 1. Whichever method you choose, cook for 4–5 hours or until the meat is beautifully tender (this differs from joint to joint, so check after 4 hours to see how yours is doing).

* Remove from the heat and allow the meat to rest in the liquor with the lid on for 30 minutes. Then slice and serve with mashed potato or warm cornbread.

Red-Eye GAMMON

Originally from the American South, this combination of gammon and coffee may sound like a strange pairing, but it works! The saltiness of the meat really complements the slight bitterness of the coffee. There are lots of theories as to how this earned the name 'red-eye' but my favourite is that the caffeine in the gravy is bound to keep you up all night!

Serves 2

30g salted butter, plus a knob extra
2 x 250g gammon slices, fat on
4 tbsp strong black coffee
Pinch of ground black pepper

∗ Heat the butter in a large frying pan over a medium heat, then fry the gammon steaks for 8–10 minutes until golden and cooked through.

∗ Remove the gammon from the pan and keep warm. Immediately, while the pan is still hot, pour in the strong coffee and swirl it around over the heat to deglaze the pan, scraping up any residue from the bottom of the pan with a wooden spoon. Add a touch of water if the coffee evaporates too fast, then add a pinch of black pepper and the extra knob of butter.

∗ Tip any resting juices from the meat into the pan, swirl around to combine, then spoon the sauce over the gammon steaks. Serve immediately with green salad or a jacket potato.

Coffee-Spiked
SPICE RUB

Coffee as a spice is no new thing; it's very good at enhancing the main ingredients in a savoury dish, in the same way that salt does. When using it as a rub, the trick is to keep it quite subtle so as not to give the meat an overwhelming coffee taste. You can use this on all manner of pork, chicken or beef dishes, and it's especially good when grilled or barbecued. Keep any leftover spice mix in a sealed jam jar in the fridge for a couple of weeks.

Enough for about a dozen steaks

4 tbsp ground coffee
1 tbsp black peppercorns
1 tbsp white peppercorns
2 tbsp sea salt
1 tsp finely minced garlic
1 tbsp soft brown sugar
5 cloves
3 star anise
1 tbsp coriander seeds

* Simply mix everything together in a bowl, or, for the best results, grind everything together in a clean coffee or spice grinder.

* Rub the mixture into a piece of chicken or pork and leave in the fridge, covered, overnight for the flavours to work their way into the meat.

* The next day, brush off any excess rub and cook the meat as normal.

Chinese
TEA EGGS

These traditional Asian street snacks are so easy to make, and they look great! Put them in your kids' lunchboxes and call them dinosaur eggs and they'll think you're the best. Depending on how long you soak these for and what you soak them in, they can vary enormously in colour and flavour. Make a few at a time, as they'll keep in the fridge for several days.

Makes 8

8 large eggs
2 English Breakfast teabags
2 tbsp dark soy sauce
1 tbsp dark brown sugar
1 star anise
1 cinnamon stick
1 tsp black or Sichuan peppercorns

* Put the eggs, in their shells, into a medium saucepan of cold water, set it over a high heat and bring to the boil. Slightly lower the heat and simmer for 15 minutes. Leave the eggs to cool completely in the water.

* Remove the eggs from the water and squeeze them gently so that they crack all over like crazy paving, but without peeling away the shell.

* Put all the other ingredients in the pan, add the cracked eggs, cover with cold water and bring to the boil once more. Reduce the heat and simmer for 15–20 minutes, then turn off the heat and leave to cool completely again. Once cool, peel off the eggshells and enjoy! (I like to eat these with Chinese roasted pork and noodles.)

Soy & Honey
TEA-SMOKED CHICKEN

You don't need any specialist equipment to do your own home smoking, just a bit of care and good ventilation! It produces unbelievably tender, flavoursome meat, so is well worth the effort and lingering smell. Experiment with different teas for countless variations on this surprisingly simple dish.

Serves 2

FOR THE MARINADE

5 tbsp soy sauce

5 tbsp honey

1 garlic clove, finely crushed

1 small knob of fresh root ginger, peeled and grated

½ tsp Chinese five spice

A slug of dry sherry

FOR THE EGG-FRIED RICE

275g uncooked rice (or 500g cooked)

120g frozen peas

Vegetable oil, for cooking

2 eggs, beaten

1–2 tsp sesame oil

Salt

FOR THE CHICKEN

2 skinless chicken breasts

150g uncooked rice

150g demerara sugar

50g loose-leaf tea, such as black tea or lapsang souchong

2 spring onions, shredded, to garnish

* Mix all the marinade ingredients together in a container with a lid, add the chicken and put in the fridge to marinate for a few hours – the longer the better.

* Next begin the egg-fried rice. If starting from scratch with uncooked rice, place it in a saucepan of water and cook according to the packet instructions, then leave to cool completely.

* Now it's time to smoke the chicken. Line a roasting tin with foil and scatter the remaining uncooked rice, the sugar and tea leaves over the base. Place on the hob over a high heat, to get the tea to start smoking and releasing its aroma. Once it's begun smoking, turn down the heat a bit. This is a gentle process – you're not trying to start a fire!

* Sit a wire rack over the tin, remove the chicken from the marinade and place it on the rack. Seal up the whole thing by covering with another inverted tin or some loose foil. This cooking process creates a lot of smoke, so open the windows ➡

➡ CONTINUED FROM OVERLEAF

and remove your nicest clothes before they start smelling like an ashtray! Keep an eye on proceedings but leave the tin undisturbed for around 15 minutes. After this time, turn off the heat but keep the rack covered for another 8 minutes, to let the chicken finish cooking as it cools.

* To finish the egg-fried rice, drop the peas into a saucepan of boiling water and cook for just 1 minute, then plunge them into a bowl of cold water.

* Heat a large frying pan or wok over a high heat, add a tablespoon of vegetable oil, then throw in the cold cooked rice (not the rice used for the smoking!) and toss for a few minutes until hot. Drain the peas and add to the pan, season with salt and continue to cook over a fierce heat for another 3–4 minutes.

* Mix the beaten eggs with the sesame oil and pour into the pan, mixing as you go. As soon as the egg is set, tip the egg-fried rice out of the pan onto plates and top with the smoked chicken.

* If you have any marinade left over from the chicken, bring it to the boil in a small pan for a minute or so, then spoon it over the meat. Finally, garnish with the shredded spring onions. Delicious.

Jasmine Tea
RICE

A few tea leaves thrown into the pot while cooking something as simple as rice will enhance the flavour no end. Play around with different varieties of tea, but be careful not to add too much or the rice can become rather bitter. This is good served with my Sweet and Sour Fish (page 42) or with Pork Ribs in Cardamom and Stout (page 191).

Enough for 2

1 tbsp jasmine tea leaves
250g jasmine rice
2 tsp salt

* Bring 1.5 litres of water to the boil in a large saucepan over a high heat, add the tea leaves and allow to infuse for 5 minutes. Remove from the heat and strain the liquid through a sieve into a jug.

* Place the rice and salt into the empty pan and pour the tea-infused water back in over them. Bring this to the boil over a high heat, then turn the heat down and simmer for 15 minutes or so until the rice is cooked. Drain and serve.

Coffee & Hazelnut
FUDGE

This is a darn sight better than the variety you will find in tourist shops by the seaside. You need a sugar thermometer for this recipe. (The photo also shows Espresso Meringue Bites – see page 77)

Makes 25–30 squares

400g caster sugar
300ml milk
100g salted butter
3 tbsp Camp coffee essence (ask your mother!)
100g toasted hazelnuts, chopped

* Line an 18cm square baking tin with non-stick baking paper.

* Bring the sugar, milk and butter to the boil in a medium saucepan over a high heat and boil for around 15–20 minutes until it reaches 115°C on a sugar thermometer. Do not stir or disturb the mixture at all during this time.

* Remove from the heat immediately and throw in the coffee essence and three-quarters of the nuts. Beat for 5 minutes or so until cooled and thickened.

* Pour the fudge into the lined baking tin, sprinkle with the rest of the nuts and chill for a few hours, or ideally overnight. Once set, you can cut the fudge into all sorts of jaunty shapes (or go for squares if you're feeling unimaginative!).

TEABREAD

This classic cake is great eaten still warm from the oven, with a cup of tea. But with a bit of imagination, a few roasted plums, a spoonful or two of warm honey or maple syrup and some clotted cream, you'll suddenly have a cracking dessert! Start this recipe a day in advance to let the dried fruit soak to its full potential.

Serves 6–8

225g raisins
225g sultanas
300ml hot black tea
Salted butter, for greasing and serving
200g granulated sugar
450g self-raising flour
1 tbsp golden syrup
1 egg, beaten
2 tsp mixed spice
3 tbsp milk, if needed

* Combine the raisins and sultanas in a large mixing bowl and pour over the hot black tea. Cover and leave overnight to soak. Don't be impatient, or they won't taste as good.

* Next day, preheat the oven to 180°C/160°C fan/Gas 4. Grease a 900g loaf tin with butter (or use a non-stick tin).

* Add the sugar, flour, golden syrup, egg and mixed spice to the soaked fruit and stir to combine well. Add the milk if needed, to make a dropping consistency.

* Tip the mixture into the prepared loaf tin and bake for 1 hour, or until a skewer comes out of the centre cleanly with no uncooked mixture stuck to it. Leave to cool in the tin for a bit then transfer to a wire rack to cool completely.

* When cool enough to handle, cut thick slices of the tealoaf and spread with lots of salted butter, then invite the vicar over and eat with a nice cup of tea. (Or see the introduction above for a more lavish serving suggestion!)

Espresso, Pecan & Walnut
MERINGUE BITES

These are halfway between a meringue and a cookie. The coffee gives them colour and makes them taste amazing. They're the perfect late-night snack, especially if you're trying to keep your eyes propped open!
See the photo on page 75.

Makes about 20

2 egg whites
100g caster sugar
Generous pinch of salt
60g walnuts, roughly chopped
60g pecans, roughly chopped
4 tbsp ground coffee
Pinch of grated nutmeg

* Preheat the oven to 160°C/140°C fan/Gas 3.

* Using an electric whisk, beat the egg whites in a large clean bowl with the sugar and salt until they form stiff peaks.

* In a separate bowl, mix the rest of the ingredients together. Gently fold the dry ingredients into the whisked egg whites, being careful not to knock out too much of the air.

* Spoon heaped teaspoons of the mixture onto a non-stick baking sheet and bake in the oven for around 20 minutes, until set. Leave to cool a little on the sheet, them transfer them to a wire rack to cool completely. These are great served with the Coffee and Hazelnut Fudge on page 74.

TIRAMISU SOUFFLÉ

This has all the qualities of a classic tiramisu but it's just a bit lighter. I know some people are intimidated by the idea of making soufflé, but have a go – they are just temperamental eggs, that's all! To make sure yours rise nice and high, be as gentle as possible when folding the egg whites, remember to wipe any drips off the edges of the ramekins, and be ready to serve up the very second these beauties leave the oven.

Makes 4

50g butter, melted

Cocoa powder, for dusting

8 savoiardi biscuits or sponge fingers

50ml Amaretto, plus extra to serve (optional)

1 cup strong black coffee or a couple of espressos

3 egg yolks and 5 egg whites

50g caster sugar, plus 1 tsp extra

15g plain flour

10g cornflour

2 tsp Camp coffee essence (ask your mother)

1 tsp ground coffee

250ml milk

* Preheat the oven to 200°C/180°C fan/Gas 6 and place a flat baking sheet in the oven to heat up.

* Brush the insides of four (ovenproof) coffee cups or ramekins with the melted butter and dust them generously with cocoa powder. Put in the fridge to chill.

* Break up the biscuits or sponge fingers into the bottom of each cup and douse with the Amaretto and the black coffee.

* In a clean, dry bowl, whisk the egg yolks and caster sugar together with the flour and cornflour until pale and thick. Then gently stir in the coffee essence and ground coffee until evenly mixed.

* Bring the milk to the boil in a small saucepan and pour onto the egg mixture. Stir well to combine and then pour it back into the saucepan. Heat over a gentle heat, stirring or whisking constantly for a minute or so until thick and custardy. Set aside to cool a little. Cover the top of the custard with a layer of cling film to prevent a skin from forming. ➡

➡ CONTINUED FROM OVERLEAF

✳ In another large, clean, dry bowl, whisk the egg whites until they form stiff peaks, add the extra teaspoon of sugar and continue whisking until stiff and glossy.

✳ Scrape a third of the egg white mixture into the coffee custard and fold in gently to loosen the custard. Then carefully fold in the rest of the egg whites, being careful not to knock out the air.

✳ Fill the cups or ramekins with the mixture, smooth the top of each and run a finger around the inside rim to wipe any mixture away from the edge (this ensures even rising in the oven). Immediately put them into the oven on the hot baking sheet. Now leave them alone and bite your nails for about 15 minutes, in the hope that they will rise and your dessert will be a triumph!

✳ When ready, whisk them out of the oven and onto saucers or serving plates and serve immediately. To really finish these off in style, dust with cocoa powder and serve with coffee or a glass of iced Amaretto.

Tea Custard BRÛLÉE

This is a British twist on a French classic. Brûlée is one of my desert-island dishes when done properly (if not, it's just sweet scrambled eggs!). The trick is to cook at a super-low temperature and then take the puddings out of the oven when they still have a slight wobble. They make a very elegant end to any meal, particularly these tea-infused ones.

Serves 4

50ml milk
450ml double cream
5 English Breakfast teabags
5 egg yolks
200g caster sugar, plus extra to serve

* Preheat the oven to 120°C/100°C fan/Gas ½.

* First, pour the milk and double cream into a pan set over a low heat, add the teabags and allow to infuse for about 10 minutes, so that the cream takes on the taste of the tea. Then remove the teabags and discard.

* In a large bowl, mix together the egg yolks and sugar and pour in the hot cream mixture through a sieve. Stir to combine, then pour this mixture through the sieve into four ramekins placed on a baking sheet.

* Place the sheet of ramekins in the oven and cook very gently for 25–30 minutes, depending on the depth of the mixture. There should remain a slight wobble in the middle as they come out. Leave to cool and then place in the fridge for a few hours, or overnight, until set.

* When ready to serve, lightly sprinkle the top of each with some more caster sugar and caramelise it carefully with a cook's blowtorch. Allow the molten caramel to cool, then serve the brûlées straight away.

Coffee & Tia Maria
JELLY
WITH CREAM AND CHOCOLATE

Kill two birds with one stone by giving your guests dessert and coffee rolled into one. Be as liberal as you like with the Tia Maria.

Makes 6–8

4 gelatine leaves
500ml strong black coffee
3–4 tbsp dark brown sugar
About 150ml Tia Maria
A few tbsp whole coffee beans (if you can get hold of them)
250ml double cream
1 tbsp icing sugar
Grated chocolate, to decorate

* Put the gelatine in a small bowl and cover with cold water to soften. When flexible, remove the gelatine from the water and carefully squeeze out any excess liquid.

* Meanwhile, make the coffee, preferably in a cafetiere, and leave to brew. When it is ready and still hot, stir in the sugar and gelatine to dissolve. Add the Tia Maria, reducing the amount a little if you'd prefer the jelly less strong.

* Drop three or four coffee beans into each of your serving cups or glasses (reserving some beans for decoration), then pour over the coffee mixture and chill until set – this will take a few hours.

* When almost set, whip the cream and icing sugar together to form soft peaks (basically until the whisk leaves a ribbon-like trail). Remove the soft-set jelly from the fridge, swirl the cream over the top in a cappuccino fashion and sprinkle over some coffee beans and grated chocolate. Voila, coffee trickery!

Coffee & Walnut
BATTENBERG CAKE

This grown-up variation of the classic pink-and-white treat is even more delicious and looks rather more sophisticated. Ideally you need a Battenberg tin, which is a rectangular tin divided into equal parts. Otherwise, you can get crafty and use folded baking parchment to divide a square cake tin in half, but it's a pain – I'd cook something else if I were you!

Feeds 6–8

175g salted butter, softened

175g caster sugar

3 eggs

175g self-raising flour, plus extra if needed

50ml milk, plus extra if needed

A drop or two of vanilla extract

50g walnuts, chopped

1 tbsp Camp coffee essence (ask your mother!)

About 250g apricot jam

350g ready-rolled marzipan

∗ Preheat the oven to 180°C/160°C fan/Gas 4. In a mixing bowl, beat the butter and sugar together for 10 minutes until soft and pale. Gradually beat in the eggs and then gently stir in the flour. Fold in the milk to create a loose, pourable consistency, adding a little more if you need. Then add the vanilla extract.

∗ Divide the cake mix in half and spoon one portion into half of the divided cake tin. Stir the walnuts into the remaining mix in the bowl and add the coffee essence. Mix well and add a little more flour if it begins to curdle. Spoon into the other half of the tin. Bake in the oven for 15–20 minutes until a skewer inserted into the centre of the cake comes out clean with no uncooked mixture on it.

∗ Allow the cake to cool in the tin sat on a wire rack. Once cool, remove and trim the sponges so they are all the same length. If your tin produced two sponges, cut them both in half lengthways so you have four pieces.

∗ Melt the apricot jam with a splash of water in a small saucepan over a low heat. Brush the warm jam over the sides of the sponges and assemble them two-up, two-down, alternating them in that Battenberg way (see the photo!).

∗ Brush the whole of the outside with more jam and wrap the assembled cake in the marzipan. Trim the ends of the marzipan, press the cake firmly together – and that's it, really. Shop-bought Battenberg will never be quite the same again!

Chocolate & Coffee
MOUSSE
WITH SICHUAN PEPPER

Now, this sounds a bit odd and you may not want to try it on your more conservative family members, as the Sichuan peppercorns are a rather tingly experience. Pepper works with chocolate really well, and gives this mousse some welcome warmth. Feel free to use regular black peppercorns instead of Sichuan, but you won't get quite the same numbing kick.

Serves 6

**2 tsp toasted Sichuan peppercorns,
plus a little extra to serve**
225g dark chocolate, broken up
250ml double cream, plus optional extra to serve
1 tbsp Camp coffee essence (ask your mother!)
3 egg whites
2 tbsp caster sugar

* Crush or grind the peppercorns finely in a pestle and mortar or a coffee grinder.

* Place the dark chocolate pieces into a heatproof bowl. Bring the cream, ground peppercorns and coffee essence to the boil in a saucepan set over a high heat, then pour the hot mixture onto the chocolate pieces and stir to melt. Once melted and smooth, set aside to cool slightly.

* In a clean, dry bowl, whisk the egg whites until they form peaks, then add the sugar and whisk again until stiff. Carefully fold through the chocolate mixture, making sure no visible egg white remains. Spoon the mixture into fancy glasses and place in the fridge to chill.

* Take the mousses out of the fridge a good 45 minutes before you want to eat them, then leave at room temperature, otherwise they will be rock hard. Serve with a sprinkling of ground Sichuan pepper and more double cream if you wish.

Earl Grey CHOCOLATE & PRUNE POT

Some people are weird about prunes, which I've never really understood. They're bloody good for you and taste delicious when soaked in gorgeous flavours – or smothered with loads of chocolate. There are so many layers of flavour in this dish, with the tea, orange and chocolate all working in harmony together – each mouthful needs serious analysis! Start this a day in advance to let the prunes soak up all the zesty tea flavour.

Makes 6–8 pots

About 24 dried prunes
Grated zest of 1 orange
3 Earl Grey teabags
225ml milk
450g dark chocolate, broken up
700ml double cream
4 egg yolks
100g icing sugar

* Put the prunes in a heatproof bowl with the orange zest and one of the teabags and pour over enough hot water to cover. Let them sit, preferably for a day, to fully plump up and absorb the tea and citrus flavours.

* The next day, infuse the remaining two teabags in the milk in a saucepan set over a medium heat. Place the chocolate pieces in a large heatproof bowl, then bring the cream to the boil in another small pan. Pour the hot cream over the chocolate and stir gently to melt.

* Beat the yolks and icing sugar together in a separate bowl. Remove the teabags from the hot milk and pour the infused milk over the yolks and sugar, mix together, then combine with the melted chocolate.

* Take your pots, ramekins or teacups and place a couple of the soaked prunes in the bottom of each. Pour over the chocolate mixture and chill until set, which will take a good few hours. Serve with a prune or two on top.

Green Tea
PANCAKES

Japanese green tea powder is a bit of an acquired taste. It has a very slight grassiness that certainly takes some getting used to, but I think it's delicious. It is basically very finely ground green tea leaves with an intense bright green colour. And, to make you feel better about eating pancakes for breakfast, it is also considered a superfood! You do need the powder for this, rather than trying to grind a few green tea teabags – they're not the same thing.

Serves 4

150g plain flour
1 tsp baking powder
2 tsp caster sugar
1 tsp matcha (green tea) powder
1 egg, beaten
160ml milk
50g salted butter
Sliced banana, a handful of fresh blueberries
and maple syrup, to serve

* Sift the flour, baking powder, sugar and matcha powder into a mixing bowl, make a hole in the centre and pour in the egg and milk. Gradually mix with the dry ingredients to form a batter.

* Melt the butter in a non-stick frying pan over a medium heat. Spoon in some of the batter and let the pancake cook gently on one side for about 2 minutes, then flip it over and give it another 2 minutes or so until fully cooked.

* Remove to a plate and keep warm while you cook the rest. Serve warm with sliced banana, fresh blueberries and a drizzle of maple syrup.

Panettone
COFFEE TORTE

I love a panettone, although they can be a bit pricy and often hard to find except around Christmas. Laced with Amaretto, lots of cream, coffee and sugar, this is an impressive dinner-party dessert or a rich alternative birthday cake.

Serves 10–12

1 large fruit or chocolate panettone
200ml hot, freshly made, strong coffee
25g caster sugar
100ml Amaretto
500ml double cream
500g cream cheese
100g icing sugar
5 tbsp cocoa powder
200g lump of dark chocolate, grated
3 tbsp instant coffee powder

* Slice the panettone horizontally into three layers. Mix the coffee, sugar and Amaretto together and use it to liberally baste each slice of the panettone.
* Whip the double cream until it falls in thick ribbons, then beat in the cream cheese and icing sugar.
* Begin layering the panettone slices back together, sandwiching each slice with the cream cheese mixture, a dusting of cocoa powder, and a sprinkling of grated chocolate and coffee powder. Chill for a few hours before cutting.

To the uninitiated, cream cheese may be one supermarket staple that seems destined to go no further than onto toast or into sandwiches (even if you do steal spoonfuls of the stuff as you do the spreading). However, cream cheese is a very important cooking ingredient, even to five-star chefs. It's clever old stuff, really, and works wonders in both sweet and savoury dishes, equally happy seasoned with a little garlic and a few herbs as it is sweetened with icing sugar and vanilla. At the very least, without cream cheese, we would never have cheesecake – try my classic American one (page 110). See what it brings to established favourites such as roast chicken (page 104), meatballs (page 94) or risotto (page 99), and experience just how international it is with my Moussaka (page 97) and the Cream Cheese Cannoli (page 109). Anyone who bakes will know it is de-rigeur for many frostings, but you should also try it swirled over the Cream Cheese Raspberry Brownies (page 106).

As a side note: one brand seems to have a monopoly on the cream-cheese market, and to be honest that's because it's the best. All these recipes have been tested using Philadelphia, and I recommend you use the same.

CREAM CHEESE

MEATBALLS

IN CREAMY TOMATO SAUCE

This mix works equally well with chicken or turkey. It produces a very soft and delicate texture, as meatballs go. You could jazz it up a little with a herb or two if you're so inclined, but I don't really think it's necessary.

Serves 4–6

FOR THE MEATBALLS

4 chicken breasts (total 450g)
1 tsp salt
1 onion or shallot, minced or finely chopped
2 garlic cloves, crushed
250g cream cheese
1 egg, beaten
30g breadcrumbs
75g Parmesan cheese, freshly grated
Olive oil, for frying

FOR THE CREAMY TOMATO SAUCE

100ml olive oil
3 garlic cloves, crushed
1 fresh rosemary sprig
2 x 400g cans chopped tomatoes
50g Parmesan cheese, freshly grated
2–3 tbsp cream cheese
Salt and pepper
Spaghetti or polenta, to serve

* Start by blitzing the chicken breasts with the teaspoon of salt in a food processor. Remove to a bowl and add the rest of the meatball ingredients. Stir together well and form into small balls with your hands. Chill for 30 minutes, to firm up.

* To make the tomato sauce, heat the olive oil in a saucepan over a medium heat, add the garlic and rosemary and cook for a few minutes. Add the tomatoes and simmer for 10 minutes until thickened. Season with salt and pepper, then add the Parmesan and cream cheese.

* Heat a little olive oil in a frying pan over a medium heat and fry the chilled meatballs very gently until coloured on all sides, then transfer them into the simmering tomato sauce. Poach the meatballs for 20 minutes, until cooked through.

* Serve on top of spaghetti or, infinitely better, with some creamy, soft polenta.

Cream Cheese & Roquefort
TERRINE

This is a really creamy indulgence that for me conjures up fond memories of festive cheeseboards. It'll keep in the fridge for a couple of weeks and is a great standby snack; it's also particularly delicious spread thickly onto croûtons and then dropped into onion soup.

Serves 6

100g raisins
350g Roquefort or similar blue cheese
450g cream cheese
1 tsp salt
2 tbsp brandy
1 tsp fresh thyme leaves (picked off stems)
100g walnuts, chopped
Hot toast, to serve

* Soak the raisins in a bowl of hot water for 20 minutes to plump them up. Drain.

* Line a terrine mould with cling film.

* Beat the cheeses together in a bowl, then add the salt, brandy and thyme leaves. Stir in the walnuts and drained raisins and press the mix into the lined terrine. Chill for a few hours, or preferably overnight until set. Slice up and serve slathered onto hot toast.

Smoked Salmon & Cream Cheese
ROULADE

Smoked salmon and cream cheese is one of those legendary food marriages. This roulade might seem a bit cheffy but is pretty simple to put together. I would serve slices of it as part of a buffet, if you ever have such a thing, or as a canapé at a posh dinner party.

Serves 6–8 as a canapé

150g cream cheese
150g crème fraîche
2 tbsp chopped fresh chives and dill
Juice of 1 lemon
6 slices smoked salmon
Salt and white pepper

* Start by mixing the cream cheese with the crème fraîche, herbs, lemon juice and a little salt and white pepper. Taste, and adjust if necessary, then chill in the fridge until firm.

* Lay out a few strips of cling film on your kitchen work surface. Place the salmon slices flat on top, overlapping them slightly, so there are no gaps in the fish when you come to roll it up.

* Spoon or pipe your chilled filling along the bottom edge of the salmon, leaving just a small empty border between the filling and the edge of the fish. Now roll up the fish into a long sausage shape, using the cling film to help roll it. Tie each end of the cling film and chill for a few hours to firm up. Alternatively, you can freeze it at this stage for later use (it is also a lot easier to slice when frozen).

* To serve, remove the roulade from the fridge or freezer and cut into slices on the angle, each about 2.5cm thick. If frozen, allow to defrost completely before serving.

MOUSSAKA

Moussaka is the Greek answer to lasagne and a great comfort food – it's meaty, creamy and spicy all at the same time. This version has a lot less grease than most recipes I've encountered. It needs little else to accompany it other than a good bottle of red, and a fresh green salad.

Enough for 4

Olive oil, for frying
900g lamb mince
2 onions, sliced
2 garlic cloves, sliced
1 tsp ground cinnamon
Pinch of allspice
2 tbsp tomato purée
1 x 400g can tomatoes
1 tbsp fresh oregano leaves, or 2 tsp dried oregano
175ml red wine
3 aubergines, sliced lengthways

450g potatoes, peeled and parboiled for 5 minutes, then cooled
50g pecorino cheese, grated
Salt and pepper
Green salad, to serve

FOR THE WHITE SAUCE
85g butter
85g plain flour
900ml milk
2 egg yolks
A little grated nutmeg
250g cream cheese

* Heat a little olive oil in a large saucepan over a high heat. Add the lamb mince and cook until browned. Season with salt and pepper and remove the meat from the pan. Set aside in a bowl.

* Using the oil left in the pan, cook the onions and garlic over a low heat until soft. Add the cinnamon, allspice, tomato purée, tomatoes and oregano, simmer for 5 minutes then return the lamb to the pan along with more seasoning and the red wine. Simmer for 45 minutes, skimming off any excess fat that rises to the surface as you go.

* Preheat the oven to 180°C/160°C fan/Gas 4.

* Meanwhile, make the white sauce by melting the butter in a medium saucepan over a low heat, then quickly stirring in the flour to form a paste. Cook for a minute, then whisk in the milk. Simmer, whilst stirring constantly, for 5 minutes.

➡ CONTINUED FROM OVERLEAF

Remove from the the heat, beat in the egg yolks, and add the nutmeg and cream cheese. Set aside.

* Heat a film of olive oil in a large frying pan over a high heat. When the oil is very hot, fry the aubergine slices to colour both sides, a few at a time. Resist the urge to add extra oil as these boys will just keep on soaking it up and will become hideously greasy. Remove the slices from the pan and drain on kitchen paper.

* Slice the potatoes as thinly as you can without them falling apart!

* Layer up the meat, potatoes and aubergine in an ovenproof baking dish, giving each layer a sprinkling of salt and pepper as you go and repeating the layers until all the ingredients have been used up. Finally, spoon over the cheese sauce and sprinkle with the pecorino. Bang it into the oven for 30–40 minutes until golden and bubbling.

Creamy
LEEK RISOTTO

Once you've mastered this very basic risotto, you can pretty much freewheel and dream up endless combinations. Though don't go mad with too many different flavours or it will become a confusion of a dish. Here the leek and cream cheese are a nice, subtle pairing, but also deliciously rich and gooey.

Serves 2

30ml olive oil
2 leeks, diced
1 small garlic clove, crushed
200g risotto rice (e.g. Arborio)
125g white wine
1 litre hot chicken or vegetable stock

25g butter
2 heaped tbsp cream cheese
2 tbsp chopped fresh chives, parsley and dill
100g Parmesan cheese, freshly grated
Salt

* Heat the olive oil in a large, shallow pan over a low heat. Throw in the leeks, garlic and some salt and cook gently for 10 minutes to soften but not brown.

* Add the rice, stirring continually, and when the risotto starts crying out for it, add the wine. Turn up the heat and boil furiously until all the alcohol has evaporated. Then, a ladleful at a time and still stirring continuously, add the hot stock. Allow each ladleful to be absorbed before adding the next. In all this will take around 20 minutes.

* Right at the end, stir in the butter, cream cheese, herbs and most of the Parmesan. Make sure the risotto still has a loose texture – if not, add a little more stock and stir through until it has a melting consistency. Spoon onto a plate and finish with the rest of the Parmesan scattered over.

Smoked Mackerel
PÂTÉ

This is easy to make and worlds apart from the shop-bought variety, with much more texture and taste. Any other smoked fish also works here – trout is good for an interesting change. The cool cream cheese helps temper the smokiness and creates the perfect consistency.

Serves 6 as a starter

FOR THE PÂTÉ

300g cream cheese

1 tbsp creamed horseradish

Squeeze of lemon juice

1–2 tbsp chopped fresh dill and parsley

4 mackerel fillets, skinned and flaked

Salt and black pepper

Toasted slices of sourdough or baguette, to serve

Salad cress, to serve

FOR THE PICKLES

150ml white wine vinegar

2 tbsp caster sugar

½ cucumber, halved, seeds removed and sliced

1 small red onion, peeled, halved and finely sliced

Juice of 1 lemon

* First make the pickles. Heat the vinegar in a small saucepan over a medium heat. Stir in the sugar until it has dissolved, then remove from the heat. Leave to cool to room temperature, then pour over the sliced cucumber in a small bowl. Set aside for 1 hour to infuse.

* Place the onion in another small bowl and pour over enough boiling water to just cover. Leave for a couple of minutes, until the onion is a pink colour, then drain off the water. Mix in the lemon juice and leave for at least 30 minutes.

* To make the pâté, place the cream cheese in a large bowl and beat with the horseradish, lemon juice and herbs. Taste, season with salt and pepper, and when you think it's good, stir the flaked fish into the mix.

* Serve with hot, buttered slices of toasted sourdough or baguette, some of the pickled red onion and cucumber and a scattering of salad cress.

Creamy
PIPERADE

This classic vegetable dish is from the Basque region of France – the colours in it represent the red, white and green of the Basque flag. It's not a great looker once the eggs go in, but boy does it taste good. It also makes an excellent breakfast or brunch with some crisp bacon or spicy chorizo sausage. The cream cheese isn't part of the traditional recipe but adds depth and creaminess to the sauce.

Serves 2

Olive oil, for frying
1 onion, chopped
2 garlic cloves, thinly sliced
1 green pepper, seeded and sliced
1 red pepper, seeded and sliced
1 x 400g can chopped tomatoes, or the
equivalent weight of fresh
4 eggs
1 heaped tbsp cream cheese
Pinch of paprika
Salt and pepper

∗ Coat the base of a saucepan with olive oil. Place over a low heat and throw in the onion, garlic and peppers. Cook gently for 10 minutes or so to soften. Add the tomatoes, turn up the heat to medium and simmer for another 10 minutes.

∗ Beat the eggs, season them with salt and pepper, and pour into the pan with the tomatoes and peppers. Stir about until the eggs set, then stir in the cream cheese, season with the paprika and serve.

LAMB KOFTE

WITH HERBY CREAM CHEESE DIP

Kofte are delicious juicy skewers made from minced meat. They are quick and easy to knock up and they transform simple lamb mince into something out of this world. The cream cheese dip is cool and creamy and holds the other flavours together.

Serves 2 as a starter

FOR THE KOFTE

500g minced lamb

1 tsp ground cumin

2 tsp ground coriander

3 garlic cloves, finely crushed

2 tsp turmeric

1 tsp chilli powder or cayenne pepper

Salt and pepper

Large handful of fresh coriander, chopped, and a dressed leaf salad, to serve

FOR THE HERBY DIP

200g cream cheese

50ml extra virgin olive oil

Large handful of fresh mint, chopped

1 garlic clove, finely crushed

Juice of 1 lemon

4 spring onions, finely chopped

Salt and pepper

* To make the kofte, mix the lamb with the cumin, coriander, garlic, turmeric and chilli powder, then season with salt and pepper. If you want to check the taste, fry a small amount of the mixture in a hot pan, then taste, and adjust the seasoning in the rest of the uncooked mixture. Place in the fridge to firm up.

* If using wooden skewers, put them to soak in water for at least 30 minutes.

* Meanwhile, make the dip by mixing the cream cheese with a generous splash of the olive oil, plus the mint, garlic and lemon juice. Season with salt and pepper, to taste, then stir in the chopped spring onions.

* Now form a thickish length of the chilled lamb mix around each soaked skewer, roughly the same thickness as a fat sausage.

* Cook the kofte on a medium-hot griddle or barbecue, for 8–10 minutes, turning halfway through. Serve drizzled with the rest of the olive oil, a healthy scattering of coriander, some dressed mixed leaves and the herby dip.

ROAST CHICKEN

WITH TARRAGON AND CREAM CHEESE

Mixing up cream cheese, a spoonful of mustard and a few fresh herbs produces a very simple but delicious sauce for a roast chicken. It's a lot easier to make than a classic gravy and you end up with a fresher, lighter accompaniment to your Sunday lunch.

Serves 4

1 x 1.5kg whole chicken
Olive oil or butter, for rubbing
2–3 fresh tarragon sprigs, roughly chopped
125ml white wine
200g cream cheese
2 shallots, finely diced
1 tbsp Dijon mustard
1 tbsp roughly chopped fresh parsley
1 tbsp snipped fresh chives
Salt and pepper
**Fresh watercress and roasted carrots,
to serve**

∗ Set the oven to 180°C/160°C fan/Gas 4. Season the chicken inside and out with salt and pepper. Smear the bird in either olive oil or butter, add a sprig of tarragon to the cavity if you fancy, and roast for a minimum of 1 hour, or up to around 1½ hours, depending on the size of the bird, until the juices run clear. Baste occasionally as it cooks. Remove from the oven and allow to rest somewhere warm for 30 minutes before carving.

∗ Meanwhile, pour the white wine into the roasting tin in which you cooked your bird. Bring to the boil on the hob, scraping up all the juices from the bottom of the pan. Reduce the wine to about a tablespoon. Add the cream cheese, diced shallots, mustard and herbs, then taste and season with salt and pepper.

∗ Joint and slice the bird, tip any resting juices into the sauce and spoon over the chicken. Serve with handfuls of watercress and roasted carrots.

Creamy Mushroom & Crab
GRATIN
WITH BRANDY CHEESE SAUCE

This makes a great alternative to a traditional fish pie. Crab has a very distinctive taste, especially the brown meat, so can hold its own against all the other flavours here. Warm, creamy and comforting, this is perfect mid-week fare.

Serves 8

FOR THE GRATIN

30g butter

3 celery sticks, sliced

2 bunches spring onions, white and green parts sliced

3 Portobello or field mushrooms, sliced

800g crab meat, brown and white

200g cream cheese

Pinch of cayenne pepper

500g cooked penne pasta, drained and cooled

Handful of breadcrumbs

100g Parmesan cheese, freshly grated

Salt and pepper

FOR THE CHEESE SAUCE

50g butter

50g plain flour

600ml milk

200g Gruyère or Cheddar cheese, freshly grated

3 tbsp brandy

Salt and pepper

* Preheat the oven to 180°C/160°C fan/Gas 4.

* Melt the butter in a saucepan over a low heat, add the celery and spring onions and cook for 5 minutes. Throw in the mushrooms and sauté for another 3–4 minutes until they start to soften. Add the crab meat and the cream cheese, season with salt, pepper and cayenne pepper. Set aside.

* In another pan, make the cheese sauce by melting the butter and stirring in the flour to form a paste. Cook for a minute, then whisk in the milk continuously to thicken. Boil for a few minutes to cook out the flour, then add the Gruyère or Cheddar. Pour in the brandy, stir, and season with salt and pepper to taste.

* Now it's time to assemble the lot. Stir the crab mixture into your drained pasta. Mix with the cheese sauce, tip it all into a baking tin or ovenproof dish and top with the breadcrumbs and Parmesan. Bake for 30 minutes until bubbling up, then serve immediately.

Raspberry Cream Cheese
BROWNIES

These brownies look amazing thanks to the swirled topping of
cream cheese and raspberries, and they taste sensational.
Cream cheese takes on a gorgeous velvety consistency when baked.
Make sure you don't overcook them, though – the perfect
brownie is moist and a little bit chewy.

Makes 15

200g butter, plus extra for greasing	2 tsp baking powder
500g dark chocolate, broken up	80g cocoa powder
Generous pinch of salt	150g chopped walnuts
8 eggs	300g cream cheese
450g caster sugar	50g caster sugar
200g plain flour	150g fresh raspberries

* Preheat the oven to 160°C/140°C fan/Gas 2. Grease a 25 × 35cm baking tin and line with non-stick baking paper.

* Melt together the butter, chocolate and salt in a saucepan over a gentle heat. When smooth, scrape the molten chocolate mixture into a large bowl to cool.

* In another large, clean bowl, whisk the eggs and sugar until light and doubled in volume. Gently fold this mix into the cooled molten chocolate, trying to keep as much air in it as possible. Carefully fold in the flour, baking powder, cocoa and walnuts. Pour into the prepared baking tin.

* Whip the cream cheese and caster sugar together until smooth, then fold in the raspberries, crushing them as you go, to ripple the cream. Now gently dollop this onto the brownie mix in the tin and swirl as you please.

* Bake the brownies for 30–40 minutes, until they have risen and formed a crust, but are still a little soft in the centre. Cool, cut and scoff.

Cream Cheese
CANNOLI

Traditionally created for Sicilian festivals, cannoli are one of the world's greatest deep-fried sweet snacks, as well as an integral part of *The Godfather* trilogy! They're typically made with ricotta but this is a velvety variation.

Makes about 10

30g butter, cubed
250g plain flour, plus extra for dusting
1 tsp cocoa powder
60ml white wine
1 egg, beaten
Vegetable oil, for deep-frying
Warm chocolate sauce,
to serve

FOR THE FILLING
500g cream cheese
120g icing sugar
50g chocolate chips
30g candied fruit
Pinch of ground cinnamon

* Mix all the filling ingredients together in a large bowl, cover and chill.

* To make the dough, rub the butter into the flour and cocoa powder until combined. Gradually add the white wine and stir together to form a firm dough. Wrap in cling film and chill for 30 minutes.

* Roll out the dough to about 3mm thick on a lightly floured surface and cut out circles using a cookie cutter (not too large). Form into the classic cannoli shape by moulding the dough around a fat-handled wooden spoon. Press the ends together and seal with a little beaten egg.

* Heat several centimetres of vegetable oil in a large, deep, sturdy pan, until it reaches 180°C on a cooking thermometer. Deep-fry the cannoli in batches for a few minutes, until evenly golden. Remove using a slotted spoon, drain on a plate lined with kitchen paper and leave to cool.

* To serve, pipe a small amount of the cream cheese mixture into the centre of each tube. Serve with warm chocolate sauce, just for the hell of it.

Classic American
CHEESECAKE

I couldn't write about using cream cheese without including a cheesecake! A very loyal customer gave me this recipe some time ago, and it is jaw-droppingly good: dense, rich and overindulgent. Bernie, this one is for you.

Feeds 10 or more...

200g Hobnob biscuits
75g unsalted butter
45g granulated sugar
1kg cream cheese
200g caster sugar
1 tsp vanilla essence
½ tsp salt
4 eggs
Finely grated zest of 1 lemon

FOR THE BERRY COMPOTE

3 tbsp caster sugar
400g frozen or fresh mixed berries (blackberries, raspberries, strawberries, blueberries and redcurrants)
1 vanilla pod, seeds removed (optional)

* Start by making the base. Smash up the biscuits in a plastic bag or whizz to crumbs in a food processor. Melt the butter and granulated sugar together in a small saucepan and stir in the biscuit crumbs to combine. Push this mix into a 24cm round, non-stick, springform cake tin and chill for an hour or two to set.

* Preheat the oven to 150°C/130°C fan/Gas 2.

* Beat the cream cheese with an electric mixer until soft. Add the caster sugar, vanilla and salt and continue to beat (not whisk) for 5 minutes until light and creamy. Beat in the eggs one by one until smooth. Finally, stir in the lemon zest.

* Pour the batter into the cake tin over the biscuit base and bake in the oven for 1–1½ hours. If it begins to pick up too much colour, cover the top loosely with foil. When done, turn off the oven and open the door. Leave to cool in the oven for an hour or so, then chill in the fridge overnight to set fully.

* To make the compote, heat the sugar with 1 tablespoon of water in a small saucepan over a low heat, until dissolved. Add the berries and vanilla (if using) and heat gently until the syrup starts to pick up colour from the berries. Allow to cool, then spoon over the wedges of cheesecake just before serving.

Sweet Ricotta & Cream Cheese PITHIVIER

A pithivier is an enclosed puff pastry pie, and this sweet recipe is for individual ones. Traditionally, the pastry is decorated with spiral lines and a scalloped edge, but that takes time and practice to get right, so I've left it out to keep things simple. If you want to have a go yourself it is worth the effort. These can be prepared a day in advance.

Makes 4 individual pies

250g cream cheese
250g ricotta cheese
40g plain flour
1 tsp ground ginger
60g sugar
Pinch of salt
A few drops of vanilla extract
Grated zest of 1 orange

450g all-butter puff pastry
Plain flour, for dusting
1 egg, beaten
8 ripe figs
Knob of salted butter
Drizzle of honey
Splash of red wine
150g toasted walnuts

* First make the filling, by mixing the cream cheese with the ricotta, flour, ginger sugar and salt. Beat well, then add the vanilla and orange zest. Chill in the fridge.

* Roll out the pastry on a lightly floured work surface to about 3mm thick. Using a small plate or saucer, cut out 4 circles. Spoon some of the chilled filling into the middle of each pastry disc and pull up all the edges to meet in the middle. Seal together with beaten egg. Cut off all excess pastry and shape into a ball to save in the fridge or freezer for something else. Chill the pies until ready to cook.

* Preheat the oven to 190°C/170°C fan/Gas 5. Brush the pastry tops with beaten egg, place on a non-stick baking sheet and bake for 15–20 minutes until golden.

* Meanwhile, cut the figs in half horizontally, put into a shallow roasting tin and dot with butter and a little honey. Splash in some red wine and roast for about 10 minutes.

* To serve, spoon some of the figs and their juices around each pithivier and scatter over the toasted walnuts.

Cinnamon & Cream Cheese
PANCAKES

Americana in a mouthful! Cream cheese makes these plump and generous, and adds a bit of decadence, resulting in a very special American-style pancake.

Serves 4–6

250g self-raising flour
3 tbsp caster sugar
1 tsp ground cinnamon
100g cream cheese
1 large egg, beaten
1 tbsp melted butter
A drop of vanilla extract
300ml milk
Vegetable oil, for frying
Maple syrup and icing sugar,
to serve (optional)

* Sift the flour into a large bowl and add the sugar and cinnamon.

* Beat the cream cheese and egg together in a separate bowl, add the melted butter and vanilla extract, and then add this mixture to the flour. Pour in most of the milk, and mix everything together until you get a sticky, thick batter. Add the rest of the milk only if you need to.

* Get a dry frying pan really hot, then carefully wipe with some vegetable oil and turn the heat down to medium. Spoon in a small amount of the batter and cook until small bubbles appear around the edge. Flip over and carry on cooking for another 2 minutes. Once cooked through, remove and keep warm while you cook the rest.

* That's it! Pile them high on a plate and douse liberally with maple syrup. If you fancy, you can mix the rest of the pot of cream cheese with a little icing sugar and serve alongside.

Cream Cheese & Chocolate
PUDDINGS

These warm puddings are like a light baked mousse, with the cream cheese making them silky, rich and smooth. Don't write off the chocolate and cream cheese combo until you've tried it for yourself – it's a winning partnership.

Makes 4 individual puds

50g butter

**250g dark chocolate
(around 70% cocoa solids is ideal),
broken up**

100g cream cheese

4 eggs, separated

Cocoa powder, to dust

* Preheat the oven to 120°C/100°C fan/Gas ½.

* Melt the butter and chocolate together in a heatproof bowl set over a pan of boiling water, making sure the base of the bowl isn't touching the water. Stir until melted, then remove from the heat and allow to cool.

* In another large bowl, beat the cream cheese until smooth, then beat in the egg yolks. When the chocolate is cool, stir it into the cream cheese mixture.

* In another clean, dry bowl, whisk the egg whites until they form white foamy peaks. Carefully and quickly fold the whisked egg whites into the chocolate and cream cheese mixture, being careful not to knock out the air. Spoon everything gently into four shallow ovenproof dishes or ramekins and bake in the oven for 8–10 minutes, no more.

* Dust the tops of the warm puddings with cocoa powder and serve immediately.

Courgette & Banana
MUFFINS
WITH CREAM CHEESE FROSTING

These sound a bit like hippy nonsense but they are incredibly tasty.
Courgette in cakes works in the same way as carrot – it makes the sponge
super-moist and helps it stay fresh for much longer.
Cream cheese frosting is a must here.

Makes about 10

FOR THE MUFFINS
200g plain flour
½ tsp bicarbonate of soda
½ tsp baking powder
½ tsp ground ginger
200g soft light brown sugar
2 eggs, beaten
200ml vegetable oil

200g courgette, grated
1 banana (approx. 100g), mashed
About 50ml milk

FOR THE FROSTING
250g cream cheese
3–4 tbsp soft light brown sugar
A drop of vanilla extract

* Preheat the oven to 190°C/170°C fan/Gas 5. Line a muffin tray with paper cases.

* To make the muffins, sift the flour, bicarbonate of soda, baking powder and ginger together into a large mixing bowl. Stir in the sugar. Gradually mix in the beaten eggs and oil, then work in the courgette and mashed banana. Add enough of the milk to make a slack batter.

* Spoon the batter into the paper cases, each about two-thirds full, and bake for 12–15 minutes until risen, golden and springy. Remove and cool on a wire rack.

* To make the frosting, simply beat the cream cheese and sugar together with a drop of vanilla. The mixture will stay quite crunchy due to the brown sugar. Taste (a lot!), then swirl some frosting generously on top of each cooled muffin.

Roasted
FIGS & STRAWBERRIES

WITH GRAPPA AND WARM CREAM CHEESE

Grappa always manages to lift the spirits! And this recipe is really a means for me to justify imbibing a bit more than I should. The cream cheese dolloped into the figs holds its shape during roasting and retains a lovely smoothness; it helps balance out the other strong flavours.

Serves 4

12 ripe figs
250g cream cheese
30g salted butter
2 tbsp honey
50ml grappa (or preferably more)
1 vanilla pod, split and seeds scraped
12 ripe strawberries, halved
2 tbsp flaked almonds

* Preheat the oven to 180°C/160°C fan/Gas 4.

* Cut a cross in the top of each fig, three-quarters of the way down, then carefully open each one up and stuff with a little cream cheese. Sit them in a roasting tin, then dot each with a little of the butter, drizzle over the honey, then add the grappa and vanilla (seeds and pod) to the tin. Roast in the oven for 5 minutes then add the strawberries and roast for another 5 minutes – any more and the figs will disintegrate.

* Meanwhile, toast the almonds in a dry frying pan. Remove the figs from the oven, spoon over some of the figgy, buttery juices and serve scattered with the toasted almonds.

Apple & Cream Cheese
STREUSEL

With its roots in Germany, streusel is a cross between a tart and a crumble. There is quite a lot of cream cheese in this recipe but it helps keep it moist and delicious so don't scrimp.

Serves 4

FOR THE FILLING

175g dried apples
175g dried cherries
100g chopped nuts (pecans, walnuts, whole almonds, etc.)
200ml apple juice
Juice and grated zest of 1 lemon
1 tsp ground cinnamon
¼ tsp ground allspice
250g cream cheese
50g icing sugar

1 egg, beaten
1 tsp vanilla extract
1 tbsp milk, if needed
Clotted cream, to serve

FOR THE STREUSEL MIX

250g butter, plus extra for greasing
150g caster sugar
Pinch of salt
300g plain flour
1 egg, beaten

* First mix the dried fruit and nuts in a large bowl with the apple juice, lemon juice and zest, and the spices. Leave to soak for 30 minutes.

* To make the streusel mix, beat the butter, sugar and salt together in a large bowl, then stir in the flour. Remove about half of this mix and chill in the fridge.

* Add the beaten egg to the rest of the streusel mixture to make a rough pastry and press into a 20cm, fluted, loose-bottomed tart tin (non-stick or greased with butter). Chill for 15 minutes.

* Preheat the oven to 180°C/160°C fan/Gas 4. Take the chilled pastry base from the fridge, line with a circle of baking paper and top with baking beans, then bake for 15 minutes. Remove the paper and beans, and cook for a further 5 minutes until crisp. Allow to cool while you make the filling. Leave the oven turned on.

* Mix the cream cheese with the icing sugar, egg and vanilla. Add a touch of milk to help the mixture bind. Spoon this onto the cooked base and scatter over the soaked fruit and juice. Crumble over the reserved chilled streusel mix and bake for 25–30 minutes until golden brown. Serve warm with clotted cream.

COLA &
LEMONADE

Fizzy drinks used in cooking? Really? Now let's not kid ourselves: fizzy drinks are a universal guilty pleasure because they're full of intense sugary flavour! But for this same reason they also make a great alternative to straight sugar in a recipe. In America, there has long been a tradition of using fizzy drinks in everything from sticky marinades to cupcakes, and it was the beautiful Nigella who helped introduce this in the UK when she encouraged us to boil our hams in cola, and delicious that is, too. I've since found that cola and lemonade play great roles in plenty of other recipes. If used for sauces or marinades, they lose their fizz during the cooking, leaving you with their distinct, condensed flavours. Try my Sticky Chicken Wings on page 122, made with cola and, quite literally, finger-licking good. In baking, all those the bubbles help give a lightness to the texture of cakes and breads – try the intense Lemonade and Lime Citrus Cake on page 133. So, you see, fizzy drinks aren't just a hangover cure or teenage vice!

A word of warning: don't try to save on calories by using the diet versions here. If you're feeling guilty, go for a run!

Sticky CHICKEN WINGS

Cooking these wings in cola makes them ridiculously sticky and delicious – just how chicken wings should be. Don't be shy about slurping it off your fingers. This marinade also works well with pork chops on the barbecue.

Makes enough for 4

2 garlic cloves, crushed

3 tbsp dry sherry

120ml soy sauce

1kg chicken wings, thin end removed

Olive oil, for frying

1 × 330ml can of cola

3 carrots, peeled and cut into thickish slices on an angle

Salt and pepper

Chopped spring onions, to serve

* Mix the garlic, sherry and soy sauce in a bowl and marinate the chicken wings for 30 minutes.

* Heat a large frying pan with a few spoonfuls of the oil over a medium heat. Take the wings out of the marinade and season them generously with salt and pepper. Brown them all over in the pan. Pour in the remaining marinade and the cola, add the carrots, and simmer everything, uncovered, for 25–30 minutes, until the wings are tender and the liquid has reduced to a glaze.

* Serve the wings and carrots with lots of black pepper and a scattering of chopped spring onions.

Glazed Spiced
HAM HOCKS

If you haven't yet tried this modern classic, have a stab at my version – great as a main or starter. Cooked this way the meat should fall off the bone and will be the juiciest and most delicious pork you've ever eaten, and the sticky spiced glaze is incredible. Ham hocks can be bought pretty cheaply from your local butcher. Allow several hours for cooking here.

Enough for 4 people

2 × 750g ham hocks
2 onions, cut in half
1 tsp whole cloves
1 tsp black peppercorns
1 cinnamon stick
4 bay leaves
1 litre cola
Piccalilli, to serve

FOR THE GLAZE
3 tsp English mustard powder
3 tbsp honey

* Put all the ingredients apart from those for the glaze in a large cooking pot with 2 litres of water and simmer over a low heat for 1–2 hours.

* Towards the end of this time, preheat the oven to 180°C/160°C fan/Gas 4.

* Remove the cooked ham hocks from the pot, setting the liquid to one side. When the hocks are cool enough to handle, carefully remove the skin from them but leave the fat on.

* For the glaze, measure out 250ml of the cooking liquor and pour it into a saucepan. Add the mustard powder and honey. Set it over a high heat and bubble until reduced to just under half the original amount.

* Put the ham hocks in a roasting tin and brush liberally with the glaze, then bake in the oven for 30 minutes until coloured and crisp. Serve with some piccalilli.

GLAZED COD

WITH PICKLED CUCUMBER

Glazed cod is a restaurant staple and you can achieve great results at home using cola to marinate it, believe it or not! The sherry and ginger give this an Asian twist. Try doing the same thing with salmon, too.

Feeds 4

FOR GLAZING THE COD
1 tbsp dark brown sugar
2 tbsp dry sherry
1 tbsp grated fresh root ginger
1 garlic clove, grated
1 × 330ml can of cola, reduced over a low heat to 2 sticky tbsp
4 × 200g thick-cut cod fillets

FOR THE PICKLED CUCUMBER
1 cucumber, thinly sliced lengthways and seeded
300ml white wine vinegar
60–80g caster sugar
1 tsp coriander seeds
Salt
Coriander leaves, to serve

* Mix all the glazing ingredients, except for the cod, together in a large bowl to make a marinade. Sit the cod, skin side up, in the marinade and leave in the fridge overnight.

* The next day, pickle the cucumber by placing the slices in a colander, sprinkling generously with salt and leaving for 30 minutes. Warm the white wine vinegar in a small saucepan with the sugar and coriander seeds. Remove from the heat when syrupy. Squeeze the excess water from the cucumber and drop it into the syrup in the pan. Leave to cool.

* Heat the grill to its highest setting and cook the fish under it for 10 minutes or so. Just before serving, drain the liquid from the cucumber and stir through the coriander leaves. Serve the glazed fish with the pickled cucumber.

Four-Hour
BEEF SHIN

Beef shin is an inexpensive yet delicious cut of meat. It takes a little longer to cook than other cuts but is worth every ounce of effort. The cola gives a gentle sweetness to the finished sauce here. Initially, there isn't much liquid added to this dish, but the onions create a great deal as they cook out, so don't panic.

Enough for 4 to share

1 whole shin of beef (approx 2.5kg)
2 tbsp paprika
Olive oil, for coating
1 head of garlic, cut in half
4 onions, thinly sliced
4 bay leaves
Small bunch of fresh thyme
250ml ketchup
2 × 330ml cans cola
3 tbsp Worcestershire sauce
Salt and pepper
Buttered mash or couscous, to serve

* Preheat the oven to 140°C/120°C fan/Gas 1.

* Massage the beef with the paprika, some salt and pepper, and a little olive oil. Put the beef into a deep cooking pot, scatter in the garlic, onions, bay leaves and thyme. Spoon in the ketchup, pour in the cola and Worcestershire sauce, cover with foil and cook for 4 hours, or longer if necessary, until sweet and tender.

* Serve the beef warm with a drizzle of the sweet-tasting meat juices and the gooey onions. This is great with lots of buttered mashed potatoes or couscous to soak up the sauce.

Homemade
BAKED BEANS

We're all familiar with that well-known brand of beans in sweetened tomato sauce. However, you can easily make your own version, worlds apart from the beans you ate in your student days. These take on sweetness from the cola and a gentle smokiness from the bacon.

Enough for 4

Oil or butter, for frying
400g smoked bacon, diced
3 garlic cloves, crushed
1 onion, diced
2 × 400g cans cooked white beans,
such as cannellini or haricot
2 tbsp cider or white wine vinegar
100ml tomato ketchup
125ml cola
3 tbsp English mustard powder
Tabasco sauce, to taste

* Heat a little oil or butter in a saucepan over a medium heat and gently cook the bacon until lightly coloured. Add the garlic and the onion and cook gently for 10 minutes until soft.

* Throw the rest of the ingredients into the pan and stir together. Cover and cook over a low heat for 1 hour. Add a few drops of Tabasco to taste, then serve, either with really good sausages or pork chops, or just on their own with a green salad.

Chocolate & Walnut
BREAD

Using lemonade in this recipe isn't as crazy as it may seem. Its sugar helps to activate and feed the yeast, which in turn gets the bread rising quickly, and also means there's no need to add sugar to sweeten the dough. Slice and serve while it's still warm.

Makes a 1kg loaf

500g strong white flour, plus extra if needed
1 tsp fine salt
25g fresh yeast
330ml lemonade
150g walnuts, chopped
250g chocolate chips
25g butter, soft
1 egg, beaten
Salted butter, to serve

∗ Sift the flour and salt into a mixing bowl and stir in the yeast and lemonade to form a dough. Turn out onto a floured work surface and knead for 10 minutes, adding a little more flour if necessary, until the mixture becomes smooth. Place back in the bowl and cover with a clean tea towel. Leave somewhere warm for 1 hour. The dough will double in size.

∗ Once the dough has risen, add the walnuts, chocolate chips, butter and egg, and work them into the dough. Tip out onto a floured surface and knead for 5 minutes until everything is incorporated. Put into a 1kg non-stick loaf tin, cover with a clean tea towel and set aside to rise for another 30 minutes.

∗ Preheat the oven to 190°C/170°C fan/Gas 5.

∗ Uncover the risen dough and bake in the oven for 30 minutes, then turn down the heat to 160°C/140°C fan/Gas 3 and give it another 15–20 minutes until browned and hollow-sounding when taken from the tin and tapped underneath. Allow to cool briefly in the tin, then turn out onto a wire rack to cool further before slicing. Spread with plenty of salted butter to serve.

CITRUS CAKE

Lemonade & Lime

The lemonade in this recipe helps to aerate the sponge, making the finished cake incredibly light and dreamy. Emphasise the subtle texture by serving with lots of extra-thick whipped cream!

Serves 12

FOR THE CAKE

120g butter, softened, plus extra for greasing
230g caster sugar
3 eggs, separated
320g plain flour, sifted
2½ tsp baking powder
200ml lemonade

FOR THE CONFIT TOPPING

300g caster sugar
250ml water
½ vanilla pod, split
1 star anise
1 lemon and 2 limes, cut in half lengthways then into semi-circles
Whipped cream, to serve

* Preheat the oven to 180°C/160°C fan/Gas 4.

* To make the cake, beat together the butter and sugar in a mixing bowl. Mix in the three egg yolks and then gently fold in the flour and baking powder. Stir in the lemonade until everything is combined.

* In a large, clean, dry bowl, whisk the egg whites to soft foamy peaks, then fold them into the mixture. Tip everything into a 24cm springform cake tin (either non-stick or greased and lined with baking paper) and bake for 40–50 minutes until risen, golden and springy. You may need to turn the heat down a little towards the end if the cake starts looking really brown.

* Meanwhile, to prepare the confit, heat the sugar and water in a large saucepan together with the vanilla pod and star anise until syrupy. Remove from the heat and add the lemon and lime slices, then set aside for 30 minutes. This will very slowly 'cook' the fruit segments.

* When the cake is cooked, leave to cool a little in the tin, then turn it out onto a wire rack and, while still warm, brush liberally with the lemon and lime syrup.

* When ready to serve, arrange the fruit segments in a circle on the top of the cake, and serve with whipped cream.

Cherry Cola & Cinnamon
MUFFINS
WITH MERINGUE FROSTING

You can use regular cola for these if you prefer, but I love the subtle taste that the cherry cola adds. The fizz makes the sponge lovely and light and the muffins are topped with a gorgeous sweet meringue frosting, which is made in a different way from regular frosting but is totally worth the effort. The egg whites are cooked by the hot syrup that is whisked into them.

Makes around 18

250g butter
100g cocoa powder, sifted
250ml cherry cola
125ml milk
1 tsp lemon juice or white wine vinegar
500g plain flour, sifted
500g caster sugar
Pinch of salt

1 tsp baking powder
4 tsp ground cinnamon
2 eggs, beaten

FOR THE MERINGUE FROSTING
120ml cherry cola
190g caster sugar
6 egg whites
Ground cinnamon, for dusting

* Preheat the oven to 180°C/160°C fan/Gas 4. Line two muffin trays with paper muffin cases.

* Place the butter, cocoa, cola, milk and lemon juice (or vinegar) in a saucepan over a gentle heat to melt the butter and warm the liquids. You'll end up with a mixture that has a similar consistency to melted chocolate.

* Combine the flour, sugar, salt, baking powder and cinnamon in a large bowl. Gradually beat in the eggs, then stir in the cola mixture from the pan. The batter should have a dropping consistency (where it slides off a spoon quite slowly). Spoon the mixture into the paper cases, filling each about two-thirds full, and bake for 15–20 minutes, until the muffins are firm and risen. Leave them to cool on a wire rack.

* Meanwhile, make the frosting. Boil the cola with the sugar in a saucepan over a high heat for 10–12 minutes, until it reaches 112°C on a sugar thermometer ➡

➡ CONTINUED FROM OVERLEAF

(known as soft-ball stage). If you don't have a thermometer, take a teaspoonful of mixture and drop into cold water – it will form a small, soft ball if hot enough.

∗ Meanwhile, whisk the egg whites with an electric mixer until they begin to thicken and stiffen, then as soon as the cola syrup is hot enough, pour it very carefully down the side of the bowl into the egg mixture, with the mixer still running. Continue to whisk for 5 minutes or so, until the bowl feels cool.

∗ The meringue will now be 'cooked', stiff and ready to use. Spoon it on top of your cola muffins and swirl it however you fancy. For a final flourish, dust with ground cinnamon.

Rum & Cola
JELLY

I'd say rum and cola are two of the most harmonious ingredients ever brought together. No other drink does it for me in quite the same way, conjuring up memories of lost days in the sun and big nights out!

Makes 4–6 jellies

4 gelatine leaves
2 × 330ml cans of cola
50g caster sugar
50ml dark rum

* Soften the gelatine in a bowl of cold water, and when flexible, remove and gently squeeze out the excess water.

* Bring the cola and sugar to a simmer in a saucepan over a medium heat, but do not allow it to boil. Add the softened gelatine and stir over the heat to dissolve. Remove from the heat and stir in the rum. Taste it – you may want a splash more rum (or none at all if it's for a kids' party!).

* Pour into shot glasses and put in the fridge for a few hours to firm up.

Lemonade & Ginger
JELLY

Everyone loves a jelly, and lemonade and ginger always work brilliantly together. For a real kick, float a splash of vodka on top just before serving (although not for the kids, obviously!).

Makes 4–6 small jellies

6 gelatine leaves
750ml lemonade
2 tsp finely chopped crystallised ginger
Peel of 1 lemon, cut into small shards
Mint leaves and lemon slices, to decorate

* Soften the gelatine in a small bowl of cold water.

* In a saucepan set over a low heat, mix the lemonade with the ginger and lemon peel, to infuse all the flavours.

* When the gelatine is flexible, remove it from the water and carefully squeeze out any excess liquid. Add the soft gelatine to the warm lemonade, still over the heat, and stir until dissolved.

* Pour the mixture into small shot glasses or champagne coupes and chill until the jellies are set. Decorate with mint leaves and slices of lemon.

MARMITE

The world is split in two over Marmite: you either love it or hate it, as they say. If you already love it, you'll be an easy convert to cooking with it. If you think you hate it, I want to convince you to give it a go, since it's one of the best secret flavour enhancers. Even if you're not convinced, try it anyway – it's good for you! It's full of vitamins, iron and all sorts of health-giving benefits, and it's even said to keep mosquitoes away, though I don't know if that's from eating it or bathing in it...! I used to have it with hot water as a kid (for drinking, not bathing) and always assumed it was a hearty meaty drink. When I found out it was a yeasty by-product from brewing beer, it blew my mind.

You've probably worked out that I love Marmite, hence devoting a whole chapter to it. Its salty richness adds so much. Marmite Potatoes (page 146) will change your Sunday roast for ever, and it really rocks the flavours in my Marinated Beef Fillet with Tagliatelle (page 153). Be warned, though: a little Marmite goes a long way. If you use too much, you might as well eat it straight from the jar. Some people bake with Marmite, and there's an argument that the saltiness does add to the sweet, but I find it's too meaty and ends up more of a novelty than a treat, so you'll find only savoury recipes here!

Spiced Marmitey
RAREBIT

Rarebit is essentially pimped-up cheese on toast. Variations of this have been around since the eighteenth century, presumably because it's easy, delicious and inexpensive. Top it with an egg and it becomes a buck rarebit.

Serves 2

250g Cheddar cheese
2 tsp English mustard powder
2 tbsp Marmite
80ml stout or ale
3 egg yolks
1 tbsp Worcestershire sauce
Salt and pepper
2 slices bread, to serve

* Grate the cheese and mix together with all the other ingredients except the bread. Season with salt and pepper to taste.

* Lightly grill 2 slices of bread, then remove from the grill and spread them both generously with the mixture. Grill again on a high heat until golden and bubbling. Serve right away.

Crispy Chilli
CHICKEN

As long as you have all the ingredients to hand, this is very easy and quick to prepare. It definitely has a bit of a kick to it but Marmite and sugar help balance this out so it's not overwhelming.

Serves 4–6

1 chicken, jointed into pieces, or
6 chicken thighs and drumsticks
2 eggs, beaten
7 tbsp cornflour
Vegetable oil, for deep-frying
5 garlic cloves, sliced
4 shallots or 1 onion, sliced
2 small bird's-eye super-hot chillies
2 fat red chillies (the mild ones), sliced

3 tbsp brown sugar
2 tbsp soy sauce
1 tbsp oyster sauce
2 tbsp Marmite
200ml water mixed with
1 tbsp cornflour
Salt and pepper
Cooked rice, to serve

* Season the chicken pieces with salt and pepper 1 hour before you wish to begin cooking them.

* Put the beaten eggs and cornflour in two separate bowls. Toss the chicken first in the egg, then in the cornflour.

* Heat a few centimetres of oil in a large, sturdy saucepan on a medium heat until the oil reaches 180°C on a cooking thermometer (if you don't have one, just get it nice and hot so that the chicken sizzles when you put it in). Deep-fry the chicken in the hot oil until golden and cooked through – about 5–8 minutes – then remove and drain on kitchen paper.

* Heat a little oil in a sauté pan over a medium heat and fry the garlic, shallots and both types of chillies for 1 minute without browning.

* In a bowl, mix together the brown sugar, soy and oyster sauces with the Marmite. Pour this into the pan, also add the cornflour paste, cook for 2 minutes, then throw in the drained chicken and turn to coat in the sauce. Add a little water if the sauce looks too thick. Serve with rice.

Potato, & Spring Onion
CHEESY RÖSTI

A traditional potato rösti is just grated potato cooked as a patty in the oven. Usually you can add chopped ham or bacon for extra flavour, but in this recipe I've used Marmite to give the rösti a satisfying meatiness. Rösti can be made in individual portions or as a single giant one that you slice up, as I've done here.

Serves 2–4

150g Cheddar cheese, grated
100g blue cheese, crumbled
600g potatoes, peeled and grated
2 bunches spring onions, finely chopped
1 whole egg and 1 yolk, beaten together
2 tbsp Marmite
Salt and pepper
Green salad, to serve

∗ Preheat the oven to 160°C/140°C fan/Gas 3.

∗ In a large bowl, mix the two cheeses with the potatoes, spring onions and eggs. Season with salt and pepper.

∗ Brush the base of a 26cm ovenproof non-stick frying pan or a springform cake tin with the Marmite and press in the potato mixture. Bake in the oven for 50 minutes or so until golden and cooked through. Serve on its own with a simple green salad.

Marmite
POTATOES

Serve these with your traditional Sunday roast. The Marmite adds a fantastic salty savoury note, along with a deep, perfectly roasted colour.

Serves 4

800g floury potatoes, such as Maris Piper, peeled
2 heaped tsp Marmite
Vegetable oil or beef dripping, for roasting

* Preheat the oven to 180°C/160°C fan/Gas 4.

* Put the potatoes in a large saucepan of cold salted water and bring to the boil, then simmer for 10 minutes or so until just softening – check this by piercing them with the point of a knife. Drain in a colander.

* Spoon the Marmite into a roasting tin and toss the hot potatoes in it until they are lightly coated all over. Heat the oil or dripping in a small saucepan until very hot, then pour it over the spuds and roast in the oven for 45–50 minutes, turning evenly and frequently until crispy, golden and cooked through.

Stuffed BAKED ONIONS

Sometimes I eat these just as a snack – they're warm and filling but also really quite healthy. They go well as a side dish alongside slices of roast pork or beef.

Serves 4 as a side

4 very large onions
4 tsp Marmite
1 garlic clove, crushed
200g Gruyère cheese, grated
2 tbsp finely chopped chives
150ml white wine
4 tbsp breadcrumbs
Olive oil or butter, for baking

✴ Peel the onions and trim the roots, but leave them attached. Place the onions in a large saucepan of water and bring to the boil, then bubble for 30 minutes to parboil. When soft, remove from the pan and set aside to cool.

✴ Preheat the oven to 160°C/140° fan/Gas 3.

✴ Make a paste with the Marmite, garlic, cheese and chives and a little of the white wine. Cut a slice from the top of each onion and push the insides apart, and then stuff the paste into the onions. Sprinkle the breadcrumbs on top.

✴ Place the onions in a roasting tin, drizzle over a little olive oil or dot with butter, then pour in the rest of the white wine and bake for 40 minutes.

Marmite & Ginger
ROAST CHICKEN
WITH MACARONI AND MEAT JUICES

Macaroni is a surprisingly good accompaniment to roast chicken, and an excellent vehicle for all those lovely juices from the cooked bird. Buy the best-quality chicken you can afford, as you want the richest flavours possible here.

Serves 4

2 tsp Marmite
1 tbsp grated fresh root ginger
Juice of 1 lemon
3 tbsp olive oil, plus extra for frying
1 × 1.5kg whole chicken
300g dried macaroni
2 garlic cloves, crushed to a pulp

500g tomatoes, peeled, deseeded, roughly chopped, salted and left in a colander for 1 hour
Bunch of fresh flat-leaf parsley, leaves torn or roughly chopped
A few sprigs of fresh oregano, leaves torn or roughly chopped
Salt and pepper

∗ Preheat the oven to 180°C/160° fan/Gas 4.

∗ Mix the Marmite, ginger, lemon juice, olive oil and some salt and pepper. Rub this mixture all over the chicken, place in a roasting tin and roast for 1–1¼ hours until cooked through. Rest somewhere warm for 30 minutes.

∗ Meanwhile, cook the macaroni in a large pan of boiling salted water until al dente. Drain in a colander.

∗ Fry the garlic in some olive oil for 30 seconds, add the tomatoes and cook for 2 minutes. Throw in the herbs and drained macaroni. Tip in any meat juices from the chicken, toss everything together and serve alongside slices of the chicken.

Caramelised Onion & Goats' Cheese
PISSALADIÈRE
WITH BACON & ROASTED PEPPERS

A pissaladière is a pizza-style tart from Southern France and Northern Italy. The caramelised onions on this have a sweet nuttiness to them and by adding just a touch of Marmite, they become meaty and rich.

Serves 4–6

4 red peppers
Olive oil, to drizzle
50g butter
4 red onions, finely sliced
2 garlic cloves, crushed
2 tsp Marmite
2 tsp chopped fresh thyme

375g ready-rolled puff pastry
4 rashers smoked streaky bacon, roughly chopped
100g hard goats' cheese
Rocket leaves or parsley, to serve
Salt and pepper

* Preheat the oven to 180°C/160°C fan/Gas 4.

* Put the whole peppers on a baking sheet and sprinkle with a little salt, pepper and olive oil. Cook for 30 minutes until blistered and black. Leave the oven on but remove the peppers. Cover with foil and set aside to cool. Once cool enough to handle, peel away the blackened skin, deseed and pull into strips.

* Meanwhile, melt the butter in a frying pan over a gentle heat and cook the onions and garlic until soft and golden brown. This will take around 30 minutes. Stir in the Marmite and the thyme. Set aside to cool.

* Unroll the pastry onto a baking sheet and prick all over with a fork. Spread over the caramelised onions and roasted peppers. Scatter over the bacon and roast the whole thing in the oven for 20–30 minutes. In the last 10 minutes of cooking, dot with lumps of the goats' cheese.

* When it comes out the oven scatter with a handful of rocket or parsley leaves. Serve hot or at room temperature.

Marinated BEEF FILLET

WITH TAGLIATELLE AND PINE NUTS

Here I was inspired by a recipe for Marmite spaghetti from the esteemed Italian food writer Anna Del Conte. The saltiness and meatiness of the Marmite, if used sparingly, works very well with both the pasta and the beef. I've used fillet of beef here for its tenderness; it is quite expensive, so save this one for a special occasion.

Serves 2, generously

1 beef fillet (about 450g)

2 tbsp extra virgin olive oil

1 garlic clove, crushed

1 tsp chopped fresh thyme

350g fresh tagliatelle

50g pine nuts

50g butter

1 tsp Marmite

60g Parmesan cheese, grated

Large handful of flat-leaf parsley, chopped

Splash of double cream (optional)

* Slather the beef in the oil, garlic and thyme and leave covered, at room temperature, for 1 hour.

* Preheat the oven to 220°C/200°C fan/Gas 7.

* Roast the beef to your liking – around 15 minutes for medium-rare – then set aside to rest, covered, for 10 minutes, after tipping off and reserving all the cooking juices.

* Cook the tagliatelle in a large saucepan of salted boiling water until it still just retains its bite. This should take no more than 3–4 minutes. Drain, reserving some of the cooking water.

* In a frying pan set over a high heat, toast the pine nuts until golden, then add the butter and stir in the Marmite. Add the cooked pasta and a little of the pasta water. Coat the pasta with all the flavours and keep everything in the pan constantly moving. Add the cheese and throw in the parsley, and also add the cream now, if using.

* Slice the beef and serve on top of the pasta with the meat juices poured over.

Asian-Style
CHICKEN SOUP

This is essentially a grown-up version of a chicken broth drink I used to have as a kid. I've dressed it up with a few of my current favourite accompaniments to make it into a fantastic-looking dish. Slice the bok choy leaves cleanly off the stem to create the gorgeous bok choy 'flowers' to drop into the soup as shown in the photo.

Enough for 4

1.5 litres hot chicken stock or canned beef consommé
50g mixed dried Asian mushrooms
6 spring onions, shredded
1 garlic clove, sliced
1 tbsp finely shredded fresh root ginger

2 tsp Marmite
1 tbsp light soy sauce
1 tsp sesame oil
2 chicken breasts, cut into thin strips
3 baby bok choy, leaves sliced off stem
2 handfuls of beansprouts
1 long red chilli, sliced on diagonal

* Bring the stock or consommé to a simmer with the mushrooms in a saucepan over a medium heat, then add the spring onions, garlic, ginger, Marmite, soy sauce and sesame oil. Let the stock tick over gently on a low heat for 30 minutes to infuse all the flavours. Taste, and adjust the flavours until you are happy.

* About 6–8 minutes before serving, add the chicken and poach gently until cooked through. Don't boil it at this stage or the chicken will toughen.

* Remove from the heat and add the bok choy leaves and also the stems, along with the beansprouts and slices of chilli. Serve immediately.

Sausage & Egg
CRUMPETS
WITH MELTED ONIONS

Perfect for breakfast or brunch, this needs nothing else other than lots of black coffee, black pepper and brown sauce to feed the hangover. The melted onions are amazing when cooked for a good hour, but if you're in a hurry (or too hungry to wait!) just give them as long as you can.

Serves 2

3 onions, sliced
2 tbsp olive oil
2 tbsp Marmite
4 best-quality pork sausages
4 eggs
4 crumpets
Butter, for spreading
Black pepper

* Throw the onions into a frying pan with the olive oil and 1 tablespoon of the Marmite, turn the heat to the lowest possible setting, cover and allow to stew for up to 1 hour. Check the onions only very occasionally and add a little water if they look dry or as if they might be catching on the bottom.

* Towards the end of the hour, grill the sausages. Bring a saucepan of water to the boil, crack the eggs in gently and cook for 3 minutes until the whites are set. Remove the poached eggs with a slotted spoon.

* Toast the crumpets and spread them with butter and the rest of the Marmite, sparingly. Slice the sausages, pop them on the crumpets, then generously spoon over the hot melted onions and top with a poached egg. Give it all a good grinding of black pepper, then tuck in.

Sweet & Salty
SLOW-ROASTED LAMB

In my opinion, a shoulder of lamb is best either butterflied and barbecued quickly over hot coals, or slow-roasted for hours on end, as I've done here. It's slathered in a delicious marinade in which the sweetness of the honey, the saltiness of the Marmite and the spiciness of the Worcestershire sauce all work exceedingly well together. It's also good on chicken (as most things are).

Serves 4

2kg whole shoulder of lamb on the bone
2 tsp runny honey
2 tsp Marmite
1 tsp tomato purée
1 tsp Worcestershire sauce
150ml white wine
Salt and pepper
Sautéed spinach and roast potatoes, to serve

* Preheat the oven to 140°C/120°C fan/Gas 1.

* Score the skin of the lamb, not too deeply, and season generously with salt and pepper. In a small bowl, mix together the honey, Marmite, tomato purée and Worcestershire sauce, and rub this mix all over the meat.

* Place the lamb in a roasting tin, pour around the wine and roast very slowly for 3–4 hours until meltingly tender. Serve with sautéed spinach and roast potatoes.

WHITE BREAD

I'm not talking seeded, kneaded and whole-wheated artisan loaves here – what I'm referring to is good old-fashioned squishy white, the kind of bread you secretly love while telling your friends you won't touch anything that isn't stone-ground and organic. But now you can liberate the sliced white from the bottom of your shopping trolley and put all guilt aside to celebrate this age-old staple in all its glory. There are many recipes for which nothing else will do, like Summer Pudding (page 181), and even stale bread has its many uses. So, if nothing else, you can offset your white bread angst knowing that you're being thrifty! But here I'll show you how to make a feature of and get the most from this often-neglected ingredient. From Banana and Rum Bread and Butter Pudding (page 182) to Garlic and Almond Soup or Cheat's Samosas (pages 163 and 162), your squishy white is now the hero of your meal. To be honest, as I was writing this book, I had trouble cutting down my recipe list for this chapter – the humble loaf is really quite amazing and endlessly versatile!

Lamb & Cinnamon
CHEAT'S SAMOSAS

I've replaced the pastry in this classic Indian street food with squishy white bread for a smoother-textured crunch. You'll probably end up with more filling than you need but it freezes very well for another time.

Serves 8 as a snack

1 tbsp olive oil
1 small onion, diced
1 garlic clove, crushed
350g minced lamb
1 tsp ground cinnamon
100g pine nuts

8 slices of white bread, crusts removed
1 egg, beaten
Salt and pepper
Vegetable oil, for deep-frying
2 tbsp Greek yoghurt mixed with 1 tbsp chopped fresh mint and parsley, to serve

* Heat the olive oil in a large frying pan over a low heat, add the onion and garlic and cook gently for 10 minutes. Throw in the lamb, cinnamon and pine nuts. Season with salt and pepper and cook gently for 25–30 minutes. Remove from the heat and allow to cool.

* Roll each slice of bread quite firmly using a rolling pin, until thin. Place some of the meat mixture in the centre of each slice, brush the edges with the beaten egg, then fold the edges together to make a triangular parcel and press together.

* Heat a couple of inches of vegetable oil in a sturdy saucepan to around 180°C. Test the heat either with a cooking thermometer or by chucking in a small piece of bread – it should brown quite gently, rather than instantly. Adjust the temperature as necessary.

* Lower the bread parcels into the pan of hot oil, a few at a time, and fry on both sides for 3–4 minutes until browned.

* Serve the samosas alongside the Greek yoghurt mixed with the mint, parsley and a little seasoning.

Garlic & Almond
SOUP

This is a wonderfully velvety, heartwarming soup. Don't be tempted to omit the eggs; once cracked and stirred through the warm soup they turn this relatively inexpensive and simple recipe into a real treat. The bread thickens the soup and smoothes out all the flavours, just like it does in a good gazpacho. Don't worry about all that garlic; it isn't as strong once cooked.

Serves 4

6 tbsp olive oil
6 garlic cloves, sliced
4–5 slices stale bread, torn into chunks
1 tbsp sherry vinegar
1 litre hot light chicken stock (fresh or from a stock cube)
Pinch of saffron
4 eggs
4 tbsp toasted and roughly chopped almonds
Salt and pepper
Extra-virgin olive oil, to serve

* Coat a hot frying pan with a film of olive oil. Chuck in the garlic and cook over a medium heat until lightly browned.

* Add the bread chunks and fry for a few minutes until they have absorbed all the oil. Add the vinegar and quickly heat it until almost completely evaporated. Now add the chicken stock and the saffron and bring to the boil, then simmer for around 10 minutes.

* Season the soup with salt and pepper to taste, purée using a blender or stick blender, then divide among four bowls.

* To poach the eggs, crack them gently into a saucepan of boiling water and cook for 3 minutes until the whites are set, then remove with a slotted spoon. Drop a poached egg into each bowl of soup, then sprinkle over the toasted almonds and add a slug of really good extra-virgin olive oil.

Spanish
FRIED CRUMBS
WITH CHORIZO AND SMOKED PAPRIKA

This might sound a little strange, but stick with me. Chorizo can sometimes be a bit overpowering, but with a touch of parsley to calm it down and the crispy bread to mellow everything, this is simplicity itself. Wash it down with a cold beer and you could be in a tapas bar on a Spanish side street.

Serves 4–6 as tapas

Olive oil, for frying
4 chorizo sausages, thickly sliced
3 garlic cloves, chopped
500g stale bread, torn into chunks
½ tsp smoked paprika
2 tbsp chopped flat-leaf parsley, to garnish

* Heat a little olive oil in a frying pan over a medium heat and add the chorizo slices. Cook gently until they are lightly browned and have released some of their delicious fragrant oil. Removed the chorizo from the pan and set aside.

* Add the garlic to the pan along with the bread chunks and fry in the lovely chorizo oil until golden. Return the chorizo to the pan, add the paprika and give everything a quick stir. Serve sprinkled with the parsley.

Rosemary, Spinach & Goats' Cheese
STRATA

This is basically a savoury bread pudding. It's creamy, totally delicious and very filling. There are lots of strong flavours at play here but they all work together like a dream.

Serves 4

Olive oil, for frying
2 bags fresh baby spinach
1 garlic clove, finely chopped
450ml milk
4 eggs
150g Parmesan, grated
300g bread, cut into cubes
(from a stale white loaf is fine)
1 × 350g goats' cheese log
2 fresh rosemary sprigs
Nutmeg, to grate
Salt and pepper

* Preheat the oven to 160°C/140°C fan/Gas 3.

* Add some olive oil to a large frying pan over a high heat, and sauté the spinach with the garlic and a little salt and pepper until the spinach has wilted.

* Pour the milk into a large bowl, add the eggs and the grated Parmesan. Chuck in the bread cubes and let the mixture sit for 10 minutes or so to soak.

* Tip the bread mixture into a baking dish, arrange the spinach over and about, and crumble over the goats' cheese. Pick the leaves from the rosemary sprigs and scatter over the mixture, grate over a little nutmeg and bake for 30 minutes, until golden brown. Serve with a simple green or tomato salad.

SPAGHETTI

WITH SARDINES & POOR MAN'S PARMESAN

Poor man's Parmesan (also known as *pangritata*) is a delicious crispy mixture of fried breadcrumbs and herbs. It is one of those peasant recipes that has been passed down through the generations, and it comes from a time when cheese was the primary source of protein and could not be wasted or simply grated over pasta dishes as a final flourish. The fact that this dish is still around today is testament to how good it is!

Serves 4

Olive oil, for frying
120g breadcrumbs
1 tbsp chopped fresh oregano
1 tbsp chopped fresh parsley
300g dried spaghetti
2 garlic cloves, finely sliced

1 small red chilli, seeded and chopped
6–8 sardines, filleted
100g black olives, stoned and roughly chopped
1 tbsp capers
Salt and pepper

* Heat a little olive oil in a large frying pan over a medium heat, then add the breadcrumbs and fry until golden, turning all the time. Transfer to a bowl and season with salt and pepper, then stir in the fresh herbs and set aside.

* In a pan of boiling salted water, cook the pasta until al dente. Drain, reserving a few dessertspoons of the cooking water.

* Meanwhile, heat a film of olive oil in the frying pan over a low to medium heat, throw in the slivers of garlic and chilli and cook until the garlic has softened and turned golden. Add the sardines – they will start to break up, but this doesn't matter a jot; they are all the better for it. They will take about 5 minutes to cook through, then leave them in the pan but remove it from the heat for a moment.

* Add the drained pasta to the pan with the reserved cooking water. Throw in the olives and capers, toss everything together, then tip into a serving dish and sprinkle generously with the herby crumbs.

Tomato & Bread
SALAD

This is based on *panzanella*, the classic Italian bread salad. It is totally delicious and everyone who tries it loves it (but try selling 'stale-bread salad' to them and you'll have a lot of leftovers – it needs a bit of positive PR!). Use only white bread for this and make sure it's been hanging around for a bit.

Serves 4

6 ripe tomatoes, seeded and diced

Handful of cherry tomatoes, some whole, some halved

1 cucumber, seeded and diced

1 red and 1 yellow pepper, seeded and diced

1 red onion, finely sliced

1 ciabatta loaf or French stick, preferably a few days old, torn into bite-sized chunks

120ml olive oil

Red wine vinegar, to taste

15 basil leaves, roughly torn

Salt and pepper

* Throw all the vegetables into a large bowl with the chunks of bread. Season with salt and pepper and leave for 20 minutes to allow the juices to mingle.

* Add the olive oil and vinegar to taste, season with more black pepper and stir in the basil leaves. This is delicious on its own or served with pretty much anything, actually!

Ginger & Prawn
GYOZAS

Roll out some white bread as thinly as possible and you have a great alternative to shop-bought gyoza wrappers. Once fried, these are particularly light and crisp and, in my opinion, possibly even nicer than the real deal … although I'm sure that will outrage some people! This recipe makes quite a bit of filling, but it freezes well if you have too much.

Makes 15–20

150g minced chicken
300g raw prawns, chopped
1 tsp finely chopped fresh root ginger
1 garlic clove, crushed
2 tsp sesame oil
2 tsp light soy sauce
2 tsp dry sherry

18 slices of white bread, crusts removed
1 egg, beaten
Salt and pepper
Vegetable oil, for frying
Soy sauce, chopped red chilli and fresh coriander, to serve

* In a large bowl, mix the chicken, prawns, ginger, garlic, sesame oil, soy sauce and sherry. Fry a spoonful of the mix in a large frying pan and taste it to check the seasoning, then add salt and pepper accordingly to the uncooked mixture.

* Using a rolling pin, roll out the slices of bread until thin. Cut each slice into a circle by cutting off the corners, or using a very large cookie cutter. Spoon a dollop of the mix into the centre of the bread. Dab beaten egg onto the edges of the bread with your fingers, then fold together to make a parcel.

* Heat a couple of inches of oil in a sturdy saucepan to around 180°C. Test the heat either with a cooking thermometer or by chucking in a small piece of bread – it should brown quite gently, rather than instantly. Deep-fry the gyozas for about 3 minutes, until golden brown. Drain on kitchen paper, sprinkle with salt and serve with soy sauce mixed with a little chopped red chilli.

Layered Mediterranean
SANDWICH

This requires a bit of careful assembly, but looks quite spectacular when it's finished. It's also portable, so ideal for eating on the hoof. Start this recipe a day in advance, as it needs to spend some time in the fridge.

Serves 8–10

1 aubergine, sliced into strips

1 red and 1 yellow pepper, seeded and sliced into strips

1 courgette, sliced into strips

1 red onion, thinly sliced, salted and left in a colander for 30 minutes then squeezed dry

2 tbsp olive oil

1 large round loaf

2 tbsp Dijon mustard

80g sun-dried tomatoes

1 bag rocket leaves

100g log of soft goats' cheese

Bunch of fresh basil, leaves torn

A few fresh mint sprigs, leaves torn

6–8 anchovies (if you dare!)

2 tbsp balsamic vinegar

Salt and pepper

* Brush the aubergine, peppers, courgette and onion with the olive oil, and chargrill on a hot griddle or under a hot grill until cooked on both sides. Season with salt and pepper while they are cooking. Set aside.

* Cut the top off the loaf and hollow out the middle (you can save the breadcrumbs for another recipe, such as the Garlic and Almond Soup on page 163 or Bread Sauce on page 177).

* Spread all the insides and base with a layer of Dijon mustard, then layer up the fillings however you please, using alternating layers of the vegetables, onions, sun-dried tomatoes, rocket, cheese, herbs and the anchovies, if using. Season each layer with salt and pepper as you go and sprinkle in a little balsamic vinegar.

* Put the bread 'lid' on, wrap the whole loaf in cling film and place in the fridge overnight with a weight pressing down on it. The next day, cut into wedges and serve at room temperature.

BRUSCHETTA
Toppings

For these, you really need some aging country loaf rather than a regular sliced white. For the very best results, cut slices about 1cm thick and grill or chargrill them, then rub both sides with a fresh garlic clove. Drizzle with a little olive oil and then smother with your choice of toppings. Here are a few suggestions, though the list of possible combinations is endless.

Serves 4–6 as a snack or starter

PINE NUTS, SPINACH, MASCARPONE AND RAISINS

* Heat a tablespoon of olive oil in a large frying pan over a medium heat. Add three tablespoons of pine nuts and lightly brown, tossing them to make sure they don't burn. Add two bags of baby spinach leaves, a grating of nutmeg, two tablespoons of soaked raisins and season with salt and pepper. Cook until the spinach has wilted. Spoon the mixture onto the toasts and dot with spoonfuls of mascarpone cheese.

LEMON, RICOTTA, HONEY AND WALNUTS

* For this one, don't rub the toast with garlic. Grate the zest of half a lemon. Toast a handful of walnuts in a dry frying pan with a little icing sugar, then roughly chop them. Take a couple of tablespoons of ricotta cheese and spread over the toast, sprinkle with the lemon zest and nuts and drizzle with honey. ➡

➡ CONTINUED FROM OVERLEAF

WHITE BEAN, OLIVE OIL, ANCHOVY AND CHILLI

* Drain and rinse a can of cooked white beans, such as cannellini, haricot or butter beans. Mash an anchovy fillet or two with a little chopped red chilli, or a sprinkling of chilli flakes. Mix with the beans and stir in a little olive oil. Spoon onto your awaiting toasts.

CHICKEN LIVERS AND PARMESAN

* In a large frying pan, sauté four chicken livers in some foaming butter with a fresh sage leaf or two and a few slivers of garlic. Give the livers 2 minutes on one side, undisturbed, then 30 seconds on the other. Add a splash of sweet balsamic or sherry vinegar to the pan, then remove the livers and any juices to the hot toast. Mash roughly with a fork, then grate over a little Parmesan for seasoning.

FIGS AND ANCHOVIES

* An unusual combination, but delicious nonetheless. Peel six ripe figs and mash them well with two anchovy fillets, half a crushed garlic clove and a splash of olive oil. Pop on your toast and that's it!

SCRAMBLED EGGS AND GORGONZOLA

* Melt 25g butter in a frying pan over a very low heat and gently scramble four eggs. Spread each toast with a generous slice of Gorgonzola and top with the warm eggs. Twist over some black pepper and serve.

BREAD SAUCE

In my mind, no Sunday roast chicken is complete without a really good bread sauce. So here it is – no tricks, just proper! Use only white breadcrumbs, and make sure the bread is stale and that you cut off the crusts if you're making your own crumbs.

Enough for 6–8 people

500–600ml milk
½ onion
3 cloves
1 garlic clove
1 bay leaf
120g white breadcrumbs
30g butter (optional)

* Put everything in a large saucepan except the breadcrumbs and butter. Bring to a simmer over a medium heat and bubble gently for 30 minutes.

* Strain the infused milk into a clean pan and carefully stir in the breadcrumbs – this mix will swell somewhat so add half the quantity of crumbs then add more as necessary until the sauce just holds it shape.

* Stir in the butter, if using, and serve warm and generously.

PAIN PERDU

WITH FIGS AND STRAWBERRIES

Another stale-bread offering that has its roots in the hard-up past.
This recipe allowed people get one more meal out of their hard leftover loaf.
I've deliberately left out any spices, but you can experiment with
whatever you like – cinnamon works wonders.

Enough for 4

Juice of 1 orange
150g caster sugar, plus 4 tbsp extra
1 punnet of strawberries, cut in half
8 ripe figs
3 eggs and 1 egg yolk, beaten
1–2 drops vanilla extract
70g salted butter
4 thick slices of white bread or sweet fruit bread
Cream or ice cream, to serve (optional)

* In a small pan, heat the orange juice with the 4 tablespoons of sugar until it turns into a syrup. Add the strawberries to the pan and heat gently until the juices from the strawberries start to colour the syrup. Remove from the heat. While the syrup is still warm, cut the figs into quarters and stir together with the strawberries and syrup, then set aside.

* Mix the eggs with the vanilla. Melt the butter in a large frying pan set over a medium heat. When starting to foam, dip the slices of bread into the egg and vanilla mix, then sprinkle generously with sugar on both sides and fry gently until golden brown – about 3 minutes on each side.

* Lay pieces of the hot, sweet bread on each plate, spoon over some of the figs and strawberries, and serve with cream, ice cream, or nothing at all – whatever takes your fancy!

Pear & Raisin
BREAD PUDDING

This couldn't be quicker or easier to make. I've used pears but you can use whatever you like – bananas and ginger work very nicely, for example. The fruit brings moisture and texture to a stale loaf of bread that would otherwise be slung into the garden for the birds.

Serves 6–8

12 slices of white bread

3–4 ripe pears, peeled and cut into chunks

100g raisins soaked in hot black tea for 20 minutes, then drained

2 tsp mixed spice

600ml milk

2 eggs, beaten

145g light brown sugar

100g melted butter

Handful of granulated or demerara sugar, for the topping

* Tear the bread into chunks and put in a bowl with the pears, soaked raisins and mixed spice. Pour in the milk, eggs and sugar. Leave to soak for 20–30 minutes.

* Preheat the oven to 180°C/160°C fan/Gas 4.

* Tip everything into a non-stick 2-litre loaf tin. Stir in the melted butter and scatter over a loose handful of the sugar. Bake for 30 minutes, then turn the oven down to 160°C/140°C fan/Gas 3 and cook for another 30 minutes, until golden brown and set. Cut into slices and serve warm.

Cherry, Raspberry & Blackberry
SUMMER PUDDING

This is a real summertime classic. Only the British could take the best of the summer-season fruits and treat them so delicately, adding just a touch of sugar, but then wrap up the whole lot in stale bread! But it works wonderfully, especially served with lots of double cream.

Serves 4

200g cherries, halved and stoned
200ml red wine
200–230g caster sugar
500g raspberries
200g blackberries
8 slices of white bread
Double cream, to serve

★ Put the cherries, wine and 50g of the sugar into a small saucepan and bring to a simmer over a low heat. Let the cherries simmer gently for about 10 minutes until softened, then drain.

★ Place the soft cherries, the raspberries and blackberries and the remaining sugar in a large saucepan and heat very gently until the juices start to run (the amount of sugar you use will depend on how sweet the fruit is already). Remove from the heat.

★ Remove the crusts from the bread, cut into thick fingers, dip in the fruit juices and line a 1-litre pudding bowl or mould, allowing the slices to overlap slightly. Fill the bread lining with the fruit and their juices and put the lid on the mould, if you have one. Chill overnight in the fridge.

★ The next day, turn out and serve with double cream – only double cream …

Banana & Rum
BREAD & BUTTER PUDDING

Possibly the best use for white bread! Serve this warm, with a little rum-flavoured custard or thick double cream. It will keep for a few days in the fridge, so if you don't get the chance to eat it all at once, cut the leftovers into slices, fry in butter, and serve with ice cream – it's just as good.

Serves 4

300ml milk
300ml double cream
1 vanilla pod, split
5 eggs
45g caster sugar
150g salted butter
6–8 slices of bread, ciabatta is good or a simple white loaf
4 ripe or preferably over-ripe bananas, sliced
125ml dark rum (or more if you fancy!)
3 tbsp demerara sugar

* Preheat the oven to 150°C/130°C fan/Gas 2.

* Heat the milk, cream and vanilla together in a medium saucepan over a high heat. Bring to the boil and simmer gently for 5 minutes to infuse.

* Whisk the eggs and caster sugar together in a bowl, pour over the hot milk mixture and stir to combine. Strain through a sieve into a clean bowl.

* Butter the slices of bread. Lay alternate layers of buttered bread and banana slices in an ovenproof serving dish, douse liberally with the rum and pour over the milk and egg mix. Sprinkle the top with the demerara sugar.

* Bake the pudding for 30 minutes or so, until just set. Allow to cool at room temperature for 20 minutes or so before serving.

BOOZE

When it comes to guilty pleasures, this might be the guiltiest. But with cooking, as long as you're applying heat, the alcohol will evaporate, so you can have your fun and feel no shame – and no hangover. Cooking with alcohol is nothing revolutionary; you'll probably have used it 1,000 times in stews or other slow-cook foods. But it's also a great addition to sweet stuff, and I'm not just referring to pouring a bottle of tequila into a watermelon (though that's great, too …) Whether sweet or savoury, booze can elevate an everyday meal into something powerful, decadent or exotic. What type of spirit, wine, liquor or beer to use is often a matter of taste, and most of my recipes are adaptable. And adding alcohol is not only about the flavours it introduces – the vodka in my Vodka-Marinated Rump Steak (page 186) actually helps make the meat more tender, and the fizz in beer leads to an irresistible crispy batter for my Beer-Battered Fish (page 195). Don't miss my Guinness Bread either – and who can resist a good old-fashioned trifle (pages 202 and 219)?

The main thing to remember is kind of an obvious one: alcohol is strong stuff and can dominate proceedings if you don't keep an eye on it. And also, if it gets near a flame, it will go up, so watch out!

Vodka-Marinated RUMP STEAK

Vodka and steak may sound a bit of an odd combo, but the alcohol has a tenderising effect on the meat and it also helps all the other strong flavours permeate the beef. You'll need to start this at least a day in advance so that the meat has time to properly marinate.

Serves 2 hungry meat-eaters

1 × 600–800g rump steak

FOR THE MARINADE
100ml vodka
50ml olive oil
2 tsp caster sugar
3 garlic cloves, crushed

1 small red chilli, seeded and chopped
Bunch of coriander, stalks chopped, leaves reserved for garnish
1 lemongrass stalk
2 tsp black peppercorns, crushed
½ tsp salt
Juice of 1 lime

* Mix all the marinade ingredients together and rub into the meat. Leave in the fridge to marinate, preferably for 1–2 days.

* When ready to cook, fry in a scorching-hot dry pan to your preferred 'doneness'. Remove the meat from the pan and allow to rest for 5–10 minutes. Slice and serve with fresh coriander leaves, and drizzle over any juices left in the pan.

PHEASANT BREAST

WITH GIN AND JUNIPER SAUCE

Game birds go with juniper, and juniper goes with gin – simple!
The fiery strength of the gin doesn't carry through to the finished dish,
you just get its gentle flavour. Be careful not to overcook the
pheasant as it can easily dry out.

Serves 2

1 tsp coriander seeds
3 fresh juniper berries
4 tbsp gin
2 pheasant breasts, or guinea fowl –
or chicken, if you must
Bunch of fresh thyme, chopped
1 bay leaf
1 garlic clove
Olive oil, for frying
Knob of butter
1 tbsp crème fraîche
Salt and pepper
Fresh coriander leaves, to serve

* Dry-fry the coriander seeds and juniper berries in a frying pan set over a medium heat. Add the gin to the pan and immediately remove from the heat. Set aside.

* Rub the thyme into the game breasts, and rub with the bay leaf and garlic clove.

* Preheat the oven to 180°C/160°C fan/Gas 4.

* Heat a little oil and butter in another frying pan over a medium heat and fry the breasts until brown on both sides. Transfer into a baking dish and place in the hot oven to cook through for 8–10 minutes depending on their thickness. Take the breasts out of the dish and set aside to rest somewhere warm.

* Scrape the juices in the baking dish into the pan with the coriander seeds, juniper berries and gin. Boil off the gin over a high heat. Reduce the liquor by about half then add the crème fraîche. Season with salt and pepper, then stir in the coriander leaves and spoon the sauce over the breasts to serve.

PORK CHOPS

IN CIDER AND CREAM

This is a very simple recipe that we all know and love. You can't go wrong with a dish like this; it always hits the spot. If you fancy it, the cider cream sauce works equally well with rabbit.

Serves 2

50g salted butter
1 small onion or shallot, sliced
1 apple, diced
2 × 250g thick-cut pork chops, seasoned with salt and pepper
A few fresh thyme sprigs
1 garlic clove, smashed
1 × 330ml bottle of cider
50–75ml double cream
½ tbsp chopped flat-leaf parsley
1 tsp Dijon mustard (optional)
Salt and pepper
Mashed potato and savoy cabbage, to serve

* Melt half the butter in a large frying pan over a low heat. Throw in the onion and diced apple with a pinch of salt and cook gently for 10 minutes or so, to soften. Remove from the pan and set aside.

* Place the chops and remaining butter in the pan, still on a low or medium heat. Cook gently for 8–10 minutes on each side. Towards the end of the cooking time, add the thyme and smashed garlic. Baste the meat with the butter a few times, then remove from the heat and keep warm while you make the sauce.

* Tip all the excess butter out of the pan and pour in the cider. Bubble over a high heat until reduced to a couple of tablespoons, then add the reserved apple and the double cream. Bring to the boil, then remove from the heat, taste and season with salt and pepper. Finally, stir in the parsley and Dijon mustard, if using.

* Place the pork chops on plates, spoon over some of the sauce and serve with mash, savoy cabbage and a grinding of black pepper.

PORK RIBS

IN CARDAMOM & STOUT

There's a great contrast of bitter and sweet going on in this dish – a real adventure for the tastebuds. Serve these ribs with crunchy coleslaw (such as my Fennel and Apple Mustardy Slaw on page 50) and a big green salad.

Feeds 4

1 × 1.5kg rack of pork belly ribs
100g dark brown sugar
1 tsp ground ginger
2 tsp cardamom pods
2 tsp English mustard
300ml stout
Salt and pepper

* Preheat the oven to 160°C/140°C fan/Gas 3.

* Season the ribs with salt and pepper and brown in a frying pan over a medium heat. When browned, transfer into a roasting tin.

* In a bowl, mix together the sugar, spices, mustard and the beer. Pour this mixture around the ribs and bake for 2 hours, basting often. During cooking, the ribs and liquor may start to dry out a little. If this is the case, just add a splash of water from time to time. Cook until the ribs have become soft and sticky. Serve immediately.

Vodka-Cured SALMON

The age-old art of curing transforms what is in essence a rather plain piece of farmed fish into a wildly flavoursome showstopper. The vodka helps the flavours of the lemon, dill and peppercorns to penetrate the fish. It's incredibly easy and very rewarding. Be prepared for the curing process to take about three days.

Serves 6–8

150g caster sugar
200g salt
2 tsp crushed pink and black peppercorns
150ml vodka (plus extra for drinking!)
Bunch of fresh dill, chopped
– stalks and all
Grated zest of 1 lemon
1 × 700–800g side of fresh salmon,
skin on and pin boned
Soured cream, lemon wedges,
herb salad and rye bread, to serve

* In a bowl, combine the sugar, salt, peppercorns, vodka, dill and lemon zest, and spread the mixture generously over and under the piece of salmon. Wrap the fish in cling film, place on a baking sheet and press it down with a weight – a few cans of beans or similar. Place in the fridge to cure. Every day for three days, turn the fish over and replace the weight again, then return it to the fridge.

* After this time, unwrap the fish and brush off all the excess salt and sugar. Slice as thinly as you dare along the length of the salmon. Serve with some soured cream, a few lemon wedges, a nice little picked herb salad and good-quality rye bread – and obviously a few shots of vodka!

Sussex
STEAK

This is an adaptation of a recipe by the great Elizabeth David. It's a real old English classic and a great one if you're short on time or patience. Don't worry that there doesn't initially seem to be much liquid – the onion and meat will produce a lot as they cook.

Serves 6

2kg beef topside or chuck steak, cut into generous chunks

2 onions, quartered

Small splash of wine vinegar

1 × 330ml bottle of Guinness

Big slug of red port (optional)

100ml beef stock or canned beef consommé

2 bay leaves

A few sprigs of thyme

Salt and pepper

Buttery mashed potato, greens and mustard, to serve

* Preheat the oven to 140°C/120°C fan/Gas 1.

* Simply season the beef with salt and pepper, drop it into a large casserole dish with all the other ingredients, put the lid on and cook in the oven for 3–4 hours until soft.

* Serve with lots of buttery mashed potato, greens and plenty of mustard.

Beer-Battered FISH

The great British classic! Done properly with a light crisp batter, it's a beautiful thing. The secret is to make sure the batter is really cold before you use it to coat the fish. The contrast with the hot oil makes it lovely and crispy. This recipe uses a spiced flour, but if you don't like it spicy, just use plain flour.

Serves 4

Vegetable oil, for deep-frying

4 × 250g thick white fish fillets, such as cod or haddock

Ketchup, malt vinegar, tartare sauce and lemon wedges, to serve

FOR THE BATTER

250g plain flour

Pinch of salt

1 × 330ml bottle of lager

100ml sparkling water

FOR THE SPICED FLOUR

1 tbsp black pepper

150g plain flour

2 tsp toasted crushed Sichuan peppercorns

1 tsp salt

1 tbsp chopped fresh dill

* To make the batter, sift the flour and salt together into a large bowl. Whisk in the beer and enough of the sparkling water to make a loose consistency that is still thick enough to coat the fish. This really is the crucial part – too thick and the batter will be stodgy, too thin and it'll just slip off.

* For the spiced flour, mix all the ingredients together in a bowl and set aside.

* Heat a deep-fat fryer or a good couple of inches of vegetable oil in a deep-sided saucepan to around 180°C. Test the heat with a cooking thermometer or by chucking in a small piece of bread – it should brown quite gently, rather than instantly. Adjust the temperature as necessary.

* Pat the fish dry with some kitchen paper and dust them with the spiced flour until coated on both sides. Dip the fish in the batter to coat, then shake off the excess. Carefully slip the fish into the hot oil without splashing and cook for 3–4 minutes each side. Turn the fish to ensure it is crisp on both sides. Cook the fillets in batches (as overcrowding the pan reduces the oil temperature).

* Serve with plenty of ketchup, malt vinegar, tartare sauce and lemon wedges.

MUSSELS

IN WHEAT BEER

I'm a big fan of wheat beer. It has some great citrus and floral tones going on. With a little saltiness from the shellfish and the zip from the coriander, this recipe knocks traditional *moules marinières* out of the park! Simple, simple, simple – and quick. My favourite kind of cooking.

Feeds 4

25ml olive oil

2 celery sticks, diced

1 onion, diced

Bunch of fresh coriander, stalks finely shredded, leaves reserved

1 garlic clove, sliced

1.5kg mussels, cleaned of beards and barnacles (chuck away any that aren't tightly shut)

1 × 330ml bottle of Belgian or other wheat beer

Juice of 1 lemon

Salt

* Heat a large saucepan over a medium heat, chuck in the olive oil and cook the celery, onion, coriander stalks and garlic for 5 minutes to soften, before throwing in the mussels and slamming a lid on the pan. Give them a minute or so, then quickly pour in the beer, give them a quick stir and stick the lid back on. Leave them alone for another 3–4 minutes until all the mussels appear to be open.

* Stir in the coriander leaves, a little salt and a squeeze of lemon juice. Take the pot to the table and devour, making sure you discard any mussels that haven't opened (don't even think about prising any open or you'll regret it!).

Stout or Beer
FONDUE

If you don't remember the seventies, this is what people ate at parties … so I'm told! The stout gives the cheese a distinct and pleasant bitterness, which makes it a little less rich than it would otherwise be.

Enough for 4

300ml dark beer or stout (such as Guinness)

600g grated cheese, Cheddar or Gruyère
or a mix of the two, plus extra if needed

Worcestershire sauce, to taste

Pinch of cayenne pepper

1 tsp English mustard

1 tsp cornflour, mixed with a splash of
cold beer or stout

Your choice of celery sticks, blanched asparagus,
carrots, cherry tomatoes, radishes
and French bread, to serve

* Start by bringing the beer to the boil in a saucepan. Throw in the cheese, Worcestershire sauce, cayenne and mustard and stir together. Add the blended cornflour to the mixture to thicken and let it simmer for a couple of minutes.

* Now taste and check the consistency; it needs to have a coating quality, so thicken it with more cheese or cornflour or add more liquid as necessary. Keep the fondue mixture simmering very gently on the lowest heat so that it stays molten.

* Serve with a selection of vegetables, such as celery sticks, blanched asparagus, carrots, cherry tomatoes and radishes and, it goes without saying, lots of crusty French bread.

Beer-Can CHICKEN

For me, this recipe is all about having a bit of fun with food and not taking things too seriously. The chicken is gently steamed from the inside by the fragrant beer, whilst being roasted on the outside. Simple but brilliant.

Serves 4

½ tsp smoked paprika
2 garlic cloves, crushed
½ tsp English mustard powder
Pinch of chilli flakes or chilli powder (optional)
½ tsp dark brown sugar
1 × 500ml can of lager
1 × 1.5kg whole chicken
Olive oil, for roasting

* In a bowl, mix the paprika, garlic, mustard powder, chilli flakes and sugar into a paste, then add a splash of the beer, drink a few glugs from the can, and set the can aside to use in a moment.

* Rub the bird with the mix and leave to marinate in the fridge for 1 hour or more.

* Now rub some olive oil over the chicken and lower it onto the opened can of beer so that the bird is upright with the can in its cavity. Place the bird in a roasting tin and cover the top loosely in foil to prevent it scorching.

* Place at the bottom of the oven and cook for a minimum of 1 hour, or up to 1 hour 20 minutes, until golden on top and cooked through. Check to see if it is cooked by piercing the thigh with a skewer; if the juice runs clear, it is done. If not, return to the oven until it is. Allow to rest for 10 minutes before serving.

PRAWNS
BOILED IN BEER

If I lived my life in a glossy Sunday-magazine-type way, there would be a beautiful photo next to this recipe of me cooking this over an open fire on a sun-drenched beach. But I don't, so all I'm going to say is that it works equally well over a cheap barbecue in your back garden as it does on the stove in a suburban bedsit! It's a nice thought, though.

Serves 2–4

570ml light ale or lager
1 garlic clove
2 bay leaves
2 tsp sea salt
2 tsp celery or fennel seed
1 lemon, sliced
1 tsp black peppercorns
Generous dash of Tabasco
1kg raw prawns in their shells

* Put everything except the prawns into a saucepan over a high heat, bring to the boil, then turn off the heat and leave to infuse for 30 minutes.
* Once infused, throw in the prawns, bring to a simmer and when they have all turned pink, scoop them out and enjoy.

Guinness
BREAD

I love Guinness, especially when drunk in out-of-the-way pubs in the Irish countryside. Nothing slips down better – other than the oysters they serve alongside it. This is an Irish soda bread made using the country's finest export. It adds a delicious rich, malty taste without being overpowering. I'd serve this with a creamy, wintery soup.

Makes 2 loaves

75g salted butter, melted, plus extra for greasing
450g strong white flour
200g wholemeal flour
100g rolled oats
120g soft dark sugar
2 tsp bicarbonate of soda
1 tsp baking powder
2 tsp salt
1 × 330ml bottle of Guinness
225ml milk with a squeeze of lemon juice to sour

* Preheat the oven to 220°C/200°C fan/Gas 7 and grease two 800g loaf tins with a little butter.

* Combine both types of flour and the oats in a large mixing bowl. Mix in the sugar, bicarbonate of soda, baking powder and salt. Pour in the beer and soured milk, along with the melted butter, and mix to a dough.

* Divide between the two greased loaf tins and bake for 60–65 minutes, turning the heat down to 180°C/160°C fan/Gas 4 after the first 20 minutes. Bake until risen and golden brown, and a skewer inserted into the centre comes out clean. Turn the bread out of the tin and cool on a wire rack before slicing.

Fig & Port
SAUCE

This rich hearty sauce goes perfectly with roast duck, venison or any similar dark, gamey meat. It's ridiculously easy to make and can be prepared well ahead of time.

Enough for 4

250ml red port
1 star anise
A few cloves
6 ripe or over-ripe figs, peeled
Salt and pepper

* Place the port in a saucepan with the star anise and cloves, and bring to the boil over a high heat. Cook until the port has reduced to a syrup.

* Put the figs and the syrup into a blender and blitz, then strain well. Taste, season with salt and pepper to your taste, and spoon alongside your beautiful roast duck or venison. This sauce can be kept in the fridge for a week or two but should always be served either warm or at room temperature.

Sweet Sherry
CAKE

For this beauty I use Pedro Ximenez sherry, a real sticky-sweet Spanish dessert wine. It's great in this cake, or even just chucked over some good vanilla ice cream for an instant dessert. The finished cake is delicious scattered with golden raisins that have been soaked in some of the sherry for a day or more.

Serves 6–8

125g butter, softened, plus extra for greasing
225g self-raising flour, plus extra to dust
125g caster sugar
2 eggs
1 tsp bicarbonate of soda
1 tsp vanilla extract
200ml sweet sherry

* Preheat the oven to 180°C/160°C fan/Gas 4. Grease a 26cm round cake tin with melted butter and dust with flour (or use a non-stick tin).

* Beat together the butter and sugar in a large mixing bowl until fluffy and pale. Beat in the eggs then gently fold in half the flour, the bicarbonate of soda and vanilla extract. Pour in the sweet sherry and stir in the rest of the flour.

* Pour everything into the prepared cake tin and bake for 35–45 minutes until risen and cooked through. Test this by inserting a skewer into the centre of the cake – it will come out clean when the cake is done. Allow to cool a little in the tin, then turn out onto a wire rack to cool fully.

Rum
CUPCAKES
WITH BAILEYS FROSTING

Britain's currently gone baking mad and this is my offering to the cupcake world. Rum and Baileys make a pretty amazing double act but there are an inexhaustible number of boozy sponge-and-frosting combinations, so get creative!

Makes 10–12

110g butter, softened
110g caster sugar
2 eggs, beaten
110g self-raising flour
2 tbsp dark rum, plus extra for drizzling over
2–3 tbsp grated chocolate, to decorate

FOR THE BAILEYS FROSTING
250g butter, softened
500g icing sugar
About 6 tbsp Baileys Irish Cream

* Preheat the oven to 180°C/160°C fan/Gas 4. Fill a 12-hole non-stick muffin tin with paper cases.

* Beat together the butter and sugar in a large mixing bowl until fluffy and pale. Gradually beat in the eggs, then gently fold in the flour and rum.

* Spoon the cake mix into the paper cases, filling each about two-thirds full, and bake in the oven for 20 minutes until golden and risen. Remove from the oven, prick each cake a few times with a skewer or cocktail stick and drizzle over some more rum. Leave to cool in the tin.

* To make the frosting, beat together the butter and icing sugar until very soft. Beat in the Baileys, adding more to taste, if you like. Swirl the frosting onto the cooled cakes, or pipe it on from a piping bag with a star nozzle, then scatter with the grated chocolate.

Cider
GRANITA

Anyone remember cider lollies? Me neither, but I'm assured
this tastes just like them.

Serves 6–8

600ml cider (about 2 bottles)
50ml calvados
70–80g caster sugar
Juice of 1 lemon

* Place the cider, calvados and sugar together in a saucepan. Squeeze in the lemon juice, then throw in the squeezed lemon halves as well. Set the pan over a gentle heat and cook for 10 minutes until the flavours mingle, but don't let the liquid boil. Taste and add more sugar if you wish (though you should still be able to taste that appley sharpness).

* Remove from the heat and allow to cool a little, then remove the lemon halves, pour the appley liquid into a tray and place in the freezer.

* Remove from the freezer after 1–2 hours and scrape the mixture with a fork. Return to the freezer and repeat the process every 30 minutes or so until all the mix becomes granular. Spoon into glasses and serve immediately.

Port & Bramble
JELLY

This deliciously boozy jelly has a fantastically dramatic colour. It also has quite an intense flavour, so it's really just for grown-ups.

Serves 6–8

6–7 gelatine leaves
750ml port
1 small cinnamon stick
A few strips of orange peel
225g caster sugar
750g blackberries
Thick double cream, to serve

* Soak the gelatine in a bowl of cold water for a few minutes until soft. When flexible, remove the gelatine from the water and carefully squeeze out any excess liquid.

* Pour the port into a large saucepan, add the cinnamon, orange peel and sugar, and place over a medium heat. Heat, without boiling, until the sugar has dissolved. Remove from the heat and stir in the soft gelatine until dissolved.

* Pour half of the jelly mixture into a suitable mould or individual glasses to come halfway up the sides. Transfer to the fridge to set. When fully set (it'll take a few hours, depending on the size of the mould), scatter over most of the blackberries and pour in the rest of the jelly mix. Put back in the fridge to set once more.

* When the jelly is set, turn out and serve with the rest of the blackberries and plenty of thick double cream.

Red Wine & Mint
ICE
WITH WARM BERRIES

Red wine is often regarded as quite heavy and sleep-inducing, but served this way, it is a really refreshing end to a meal.

Serves 4

600ml red wine
½ bunch of fresh mint
450g caster sugar, plus 2 tbsp extra
125g strawberries
125g raspberries
125g blueberries

* Pour the red wine into a large saucepan, add the whole sprigs of mint and the 450g of sugar and cook over a gentle heat for 30 minutes to infuse. Remove from the heat and allow to cool.

* Once cool, remove the mint, pour the liquor into a shallow tray and freeze, scraping with a fork every hour or so to create coarse crystals.

* Just before you want to serve, very, very gently warm the berries with the extra 2 tablespoons of sugar, just until their juices start to run. Remove from the heat.

* Spoon the red wine crystals into cold serving glasses or bowls, and spoon over some of the warm berries and their juice. Serve immediately – this doesn't hang around for long before turning back into minty red wine!

Boozy
CHOCOLATE SAUCES

These boozy sauces are great as part of a really naughty ice cream sundae! The red wine sauce is best made with a particularly fruity or spicy wine, nothing flaccid or dull, and a top-quality dark chocolate. While the Guinness chocolate syrup must be tried to be believed – the beer adds a delicious bitter note and helps to accentuate the cocoa flavour. Drizzle them both liberally onto ice cream while still warm and get ready to dive in!

Serves 4

RED WINE CHOCOLATE SAUCE

* Pour 130ml deep red wine (such as Merlot or Syrah) into a small saucepan, add 40g caster or icing sugar and bring to a simmer over a medium heat, stirring to dissolve the sugar.

* Break up 250g good-quality dark chocolate (70% cocoa solids) into pieces and place in a heatproof bowl, then pour on the hot wine and stir together until the chocolate lumps have completely melted. Loosen the sauce a little with another glug or two of wine, then serve while still gorgeous and warm.

GUINNESS CHOCOLATE SYRUP

* In a saucepan, combine 250ml Guinness or other stout, 200g sifted cocoa powder and 120g soft brown sugar and bring to the boil over a medium heat. Stir together until well combined, then remove from the heat and serve while still warm.

Cider-Poached
QUINCE
WITH WALNUT CUSTARD

Quinces are rather old-fashioned fruits, with a limited season from October to December, so you don't often see them for sale. But with a bit of persistence you should find them (try the farmers' markets) and they are a real reward. If you're new to the quince, be warned that in their raw form they are both ugly and inedible, which is not a great start in life, but once cooked they become beautiful, fragrant and totally delicious.

Serves 4

FOR POACHING THE QUINCE
2 × 500ml bottles of sweet cider
100ml runny honey
1 cinnamon stick
2–3 cloves
1 star anise
A few strips of lemon peel
Good slug of calvados or brandy
3 ripe-ish quinces, peeled, quartered and core removed

FOR THE WALNUT CUSTARD
500ml milk
Large handful of toasted walnuts, roughly chopped
6 egg yolks
100g light brown sugar

* Put all the poaching ingredients, apart from the quinces themselves, into a saucepan and bring to the boil, then simmer over a low heat for 30 minutes.

* Drop in the quinces, making sure they are fully submerged (else the fruit will turn partially brown) and simmer over a low heat for another 30 minutes. Turn off the heat and allow the fruit to finish cooking as it cools completely.

* Begin the walnut custard a good half an hour before you wish to eat. Heat the milk in a saucepan with the chopped toasted walnuts. Remove from the heat and leave to infuse for 30 minutes, then strain to remove the walnuts.

* Beat the egg yolks with the sugar in a large bowl until well combined. Pour the infused milk over the yolk mixture and stir. Pour back into the milk pan, place on a gentle heat and stir continuously to thicken. Pass through a sieve and spoon over the cooked quinces.

Raspberry & Whisky
CRANACHAN

This traditional Scottish dessert is made using three of the country's finest ingredients: raspberries, whisky and oats. For me, the best time to eat this is late summer or early autumn, when raspberries are at their juiciest. In terms of the type of whisky you use, obviously the better quality it is the more delicious the finished dessert will be.

Enough for 4

70g butter
4 tbsp honey
50g hazelnuts
40g plain flour
75g pinhead oatmeal or porridge oats
450g fresh raspberries
1 tbsp icing sugar
6 tbsp whisky
450ml double cream

* Preheat the oven to 180°C/160°C fan/Gas 4.

* Melt the butter and honey with the nuts, flour and oatmeal in a saucepan over a medium heat. Stir together and spread the mixture over a non-stick baking sheet. Bake in the oven for 20 minutes, then remove and allow to cool.

* When cool, place the mixture on a chopping board and smash it up into small pieces, or simply whiz it in a food processor, which is far more effective. This is your cranachan mixture.

* Mash or blend half the raspberries with the icing sugar and a little of the whisky. Stir in the rest of the raspberries.

* Whip up the cream to soft peaks, stir in a handful of the cranachan and the rest of the whisky. Grab a glass or serving bowl, spoon some of the raspberry mixture into the base, top with some cream and the rest of the cranachan and serve.

Apple
FRITTERS

In this recipe, the apples need to wallow in the alcohol for as long as possible so that they soak up loads of flavour. The batter should be really light and airy, and the oil should be fresh and not previously used.

Serves 4

3 Cox's apples or similar, peeled and cut into small pieces
150ml brandy or calvados
4 whole eggs, plus 2 egg whites
50g caster sugar
150ml plain flour
Vegetable oil, for deep-frying
2 tbsp caster sugar mixed with 1 tsp cinnamon
Whipped cream and honey, to serve

* Place the apple pieces in a small bowl and cover with the brandy or calvados. Leave to steep for an hour or so to soak up the booze. Drain, reserving the liquid.

* Beat the whole eggs and sugar together, and gradually incorporate the flour. Add all the alcohol that the apples have been soaking in, and stir to make a batter. Whisk the egg whites and gently fold them into this batter.

* Heat a couple of inches of vegetable oil in a sturdy saucepan to around 180°C. Test the heat either with a cooking thermometer or by chucking in a small piece of bread – it should brown quite gently, rather than instantly. Adjust the temperature as necessary.

* Now drop the soaked apple pieces into the batter to coat them, then carefully lower them into the hot oil and cook for a few minutes until golden brown. When done, remove, drain on kitchen paper, and roll in the cinnamon sugar. Serve with whipped cream and a drizzle of honey.

Sherry, Chocolate & Mascarpone
TRIFLE

The bigger the better with this showstopper! The great thing about trifles is that they can be as quick and easy as you like. There's no snobbery in buying the odd tin of fruit or custard, as long as the finished thing looks stunning. Really good shop-bought brownies work a treat here as well … but make sure you douse them in lots of sherry.

Serves 8–10

600g brownies (either good-quality shop-bought, or made as per page 106, but with the raspberry cream cheese topping omitted)

2 × 410g tins of pears, drained

500ml mascarpone cheese

500ml double cream

Chocolate shavings and toasted almonds, to decorate

FOR THE JELLY

1 × 750ml bottle of sweet sherry

8 gelatine leaves

300ml sugar syrup (150g caster sugar simmered in 150ml water)

150g fresh raspberries

FOR THE CUSTARD

1 litre double cream

4 vanilla pods or a few drops of essence

12 egg yolks

100g light brown sugar

* Douse the brownies generously with some of the sherry for the jelly and set aside to soak.

* To make the jelly, soften the gelatine in a little cold water. When flexible, remove from the water, carefully squeeze out excess liquid, and place in a large bowl.

* Bring the sugar syrup to the boil in a pan, then pour it over the drained gelatine. Add the rest of the sherry, throw in the raspberries and chill until cool but not set.

* For the custard, heat the double cream with the vanilla. Mix the egg yolks and sugar together in a large bowl, then pour in the boiling cream, stir and return the mixture to the pan. Stir constantly over a low heat until thickened but not ➡

➡ CONTINUED FROM OVERLEAF

scrambled! Strain, removing the vanilla pod, and place the custard in the fridge to chill completely.

∗ When everything is chilled, pour the jelly mixture into the base of the serving bowl, add the pears and chill until set.

∗ Next, add the brownies, followed by the custard – though to be quite honest the order of layers doesn't matter, so just go with whatever order you like.

∗ Finally, beat the mascarpone with the double cream until thick and forming soft peaks, then spoon it generously over the top of the trifle, swirling it however you fancy. Decorate with chocolate shavings and toasted nuts. Amazing!

INDEX

ABOUT THE AUTHOR

Matt Tebbutt presents Channel 4's *Food Unwrapped*. He is also known for championing forgotten foods on BBC Two's *Great British Food Revival*, co-presenting UKTV Food's *Market Kitchen*, representing Wales on BBC Two's *Great British Menu* and stepping in as guest presenter on *Saturday Kitchen*.

A graduate of Leiths School of Food and Wine, Matt has worked with some of the biggest names in food, and now owns and runs the acclaimed Foxhunter restaurant in Nantyderry, South Wales, for which he won AA Restaurant of the Year for Wales in 2004. Matt lives in Monmouthshire with his wife and children. This is his second book.

ACKNOWLEDGEMENTS

So, a big thank you in no particular order to the little army of helpers who got this book off the ground. To the boys at The Foxhunter, John and G, for their continued help and trust in sailing the ship while I'm gallivanting elsewhere, having a lovely time! To two great friends, Chris and Nicole, for being quite simply the best food and photography team anyone could wish for. If you like the look of any of the photos in this book … it's down to them. To the dream pairing of American Jenny and Ione, for your guidance and patience with my poor spelling and tardy timekeeping. Lovely Hilary and Amanda, agents/power women without equal. And obviously to my beautiful and patient wife, Lisa, who indulges all my whims … to a point … and to my supercool kids Jess and Henry. Big love to you all. X

Quercus Editions Ltd
55 Baker Street
7th Floor, South Block
London
W1U 8EW

First published in 2013

Text copyright © Matt Tebbutt, 2013
Photographs © Chris Terry, 2013

A catalogue record of this book is available from the British Library

ISBN 978 1 78206 467 1

Publishing Director: Jenny Heller
Editor: Ione Walder
Design, layout and cover: Nicky Barneby
Food styling: Nicole Herft
Prop styling: Cynthia Inions
Copy-editing: Helena Caldon

Printed and bound in Portugal

1 3 5 7 9 10 8 6 4 2